ORISHAS

The Complete Guide to Yoruba Tradition, Sacred Rituals, the Divine Feminine, and Spiritual Enlightenment of African Culture and Wisdom

By Odette J. Toussaint

OrangePen Publications is a company of writers, designers, editors,researchers and other professionals, who have formed a team to create and publish unique and extraordinary works of literature. The main purpose of **OrangePen Publications** is to spread information and help people improve their lives thanks to indepth, comprehensive communication, resulting from years of study and research. The publications cover many areas of life - health, psychology, investing, relationships, spirituality, and more - and each area has its own author. Quality literature and customer satisfaction are primary aspects of our work, which is why the **OrangePen Publications** team continually seeks out new topics to provide content-rich, in-depth reading.

TABLE OF CONTENTS

INTRODUCTION 1

YORUBA CULTURE 4

The African Continent, the Cradle of Traditions 4

The Birth of Yoruba Culture in Africa and Its Great Importance 8

Origin of the Name "Yoruba" 10

History of the Yoruba People 11

Expansion to Other Parts of the World 13

THE YORUBA RELIGION 19

What is Yoruba? 19

What Do Yoruba People Believe? 23

Fundamental Beliefs And Traditions In The Yoruba 25

Traditions of the Yoruba People 27

OLODUMARE/OLORUN 29

ORISHAS 41

First Class Orisha 42

Deified Mortals 43

Natural Elements and Other Spiritual Entities 44

Colors of the Orisha 45

HOW TO WORSHIP THE ORISHAS 47

Simple Prayers 48

Model of Prayer 48

Ashe 51

Ebo Riru (Sacrifice) 53

Cowrie's Shell Divination (Obi Divination-Diloggun Divination) 54

WHITE ORISHAS I 58

OBATALA 59

Path of Obatala 62

Oriki Obatala 66

ORUNMILA 68

Oriki Orunmila 70

Odu Ifa 72

WHITE ORISHAS II: THE GODS OF WATER **75**

OLOKUN 76

Oriki Olokun 78

YEMOJA 79

Paths of Yemoja 82

Oriki Yemoja 85

OSUN 86

Paths of *Osun* 87

Oriki Osun 90

DARK ORISHAS I: THE TRICKSTER AND THE WARRIOR 92

ESU 92

Paths of Esu 94

Oriki Esu 97

OGUN 99

Paths of Ogun 101

Oriki Ogun 104

DARK ORISHAS II: SANGO AND OYA **105**

SANGO 106

Paths of Sango 108

Oriki Sango 111

OYA 113

Paths of Oya 115

Oriki Oya 117

DARK ORISHAS III: THE HEALERS.................................**118**

BABALUWAYE 119

Invoking Babaluwaye 121

Paths of Babaluwaye 123

Osanyin and the Differences with Babaluwaye...........................125

OTHER IMPORTANT ORISHAS **127**

OBA...127

AJE 128

NANA BULUKU 130

OSHUMARE 131

OSHOSI...131

OKO 133

ORI 134

EGBE...134

HOODOO AND VOODOO **135**

HOODOO...135

VOODOO 136

CONNECT AND TALK TO THE ORISHAS...............................**138**

Tools for Divination.................................141

DIVINATION SYSTEMS...............................**143**

Interpreting Shells' Mouths 146

Obi Divination.....................................147

Alaafia 147

Etawa 147

Ejife 148

Okanran 148

Oyekun 148

Ifa Divination.......................................148

Okanran 149

Eji Oko 149

Ogunda 149

Irosun 149

Ose 149

Obara 149

Odi 149

Eji Ogbe 149

Osa 149

Ofun 149

Owonrin 150

Ejila Sebora 150

Ika 150

Oturupon 150

Ofun Kanran 150

Irete 150

Diloggun Divination and the 16 Basic Patterns 150

Okanran 151

Eji Oko 151

Eta Ogunda 151

Irosun 152

Ose 152

Obara 152

Odi 152

Eji Onile 152

Osa 152

Ofun 152

Owanrin 152

Ejila Sebora 153

Eji Ologbon 153

Ika 153

Osbegunda 153

Alaafia 153

Opira 153

Tips for Divination 153

ORISHAS FESTIVAL AFRICA..**156**

Olokun Festival 156

Osun Festival 157

Sango Festival 157

Obatala Festival 158

Olojo Festival 159

Ogun Festival...159

Yemoja Festival 160

SANTERIA **162**

Key Points of the Santeria Belief System.............................163

Followers of Santeria Believe in Just One God.....................163

Santeria Followers Worship Their Ancestors 164

Divination 165

Two Concepts Are Vital to the Fundamental Beliefs of Santeria.166

Santeria Isn't Witchcraft 167

Animal Offerings..167

Their Temple - The House of a Santeros 168

ORISHAS IN OUR DAY **170**

CONCLUSION **173**

INTRODUCTION

The Yoruba people are one of the major ethnic groups of Africa who inhabit central Nigeria, southwestern Niger, and western Cameroon. The Yoruba language is the best-known member of the Niger-Congo family, spoken by nearly 30 million people worldwide.

Yoruba tradition holds that an early ancestor named Oduduwa migrated north from Ile Ife in present-day Nigeria with other migrants to take possession of a piece of land that was considered theirs by ancient requests made to divine ancestors. Oduduwa became ruler over this territory and established his capital at Oyo.

The Yoruba speaks a language that belongs to the Niger-Congo family, with considerable Hausa and Fulani influence. The language is highly structured and characterized by intricate rhythms (Sufi) and complex tonal qualities (music).

The Yoruba make up about 17% of Nigeria's population; this group includes about 22 million people whose primary villages are located in southwestern Nigeria. Yorubas have historically lived in an area covered by scattered small political units. Until the colonial period, the Yoruba people were organized by townlands, larger units also known as "jagun" or "okunrin" land, consisting of several small townships.

The okunrin is responsible for public works, judicial affairs, and the selection of the junior chief. However, people rarely interacted with their leaders because they were viewed as very powerful and mystical. Instead, most communication is conducted at the village level. Each village is autonomous with its unique history. Approximately 300 distinct communities in southwestern Nigeria are spread across five geopolitical zones. A collection of towns were built around a central town or city called a "lga." Lga's ruled by a king (Oba) who would share power with various councils consisting of civilian elders of different family lineages and professional guilds such as priests, traders, etc.

The king was a ceremonial position rather than a political one, as seen in other parts of Africa. The political power lies within the councils, mostly elders from powerful lineage families. In the days of conquest, warring parties represented by their chiefs were selected through a series of ingenious tests designed to ascertain their bravery and determine whether they had the skills needed for leadership.

Religion is perhaps the most important institution that shaped life in Yorubaland. It provided the moral and legal foundation for social relations and activities. It ensured that individuals and communities operated within a well-understood supernatural and natural order. The peninsula became widely known as "The Land of the Holy Spirit" or simply "The Land of Ori." Since the 19th century, missionaries have been active in Yoruba land, and their influence has been wide-ranging. Church missions were established by the Wesleyan Missionary Society, the Church of England, and later several Baptists. For a long time, Protestant missionaries influenced Yoruba culture far more than Islamic missionaries from other countries.

In contrast to most other African peoples who often adopted religious ideas from others, the Yoruba people have always considered themselves true believers in their religion practiced for thousands of years. In fact, many traditional customs are practiced today.

The Yoruba people believe in a supreme being called Olorun. They believe that he is the father of all creation and also the owner of the cosmos. Behind him are minor but powerful deities subordinate to him. There are many lesser gods in Yoruba belief. Some represent natural forces (e.g., Olokun, the orisha of the ocean; Ogboni, the orisha of iron), and others represent ancestors (e.g., Eshu, Olofi). These deities are grouped into four categories:

Between Olorun and these gods are other intermediary spirits called Orishas. Each of the orishas corresponds

to one of the following characteristics:

The orishas are believed to be spirits who live in nature and help humans with practical matters (e.g., the gods of iron who serve as protectors against snakebite). They also influence humanity in various ways. One of the most important is that each orisha confers specific skills on human beings, known as "ashé." Those with artistic, intellectual, or spiritual attributes are traditionally called Orisa, meaning "the wise," or Orisa Opa meaning "the highly literate." The orishas can be grouped by their human characteristics (e.g., Osanyin, the god of herbs and healing).

There are hundreds of orishas ranging from gods who govern forces of nature (e.g., stones) to those who exert control over social relations (e.g., Esu, the messenger, or psychopomp). Each deity has particular abilities and responsibilities. The Yoruba pantheon is vast and complex; this complexity is mirrored in the various facets of life governed by these deities.

The gods are believed to be around people at all times; they must be worshipped every day to help human beings live long, healthy lives free from sickness and trouble. Families perform rituals known as "beliefs" (i.e., the worship of Olumo Otu, god of fertility) to ensure that their gods are appeased, and that success is achieved for all.

YORUBA CULTURE

The African Continent, the Cradle of Traditions

Africa is home to various unique and interesting cultures, many of which have been studied and documented in depth. One such culture is the Yoruba people of Nigeria, the home country of the famous Orisha worshippers.

Nigeria has a large number of different vibrant cultures, and Nigeria's history dates back 3000 years to when the Yoruba people migrated from the Sahara Desert. The Yoruba people settled in what eventually became an area called Oyo Midan (The Place) on the Niger River. Eventually, the Oyo Midan expanded into several major city-states that included Ibadan, Osun, and Ijebu Ode, all growing on their own separate cultures within a larger "Ibo" Yoruba culture.

In the past, the capitals of the Yoruba land were connected with each other in a kind of open confederation under the leadership of the leader of the Yoruba people.

The confederation had as its cornerstone the consideration that the people were like a big family, and this has certainly favored peace and harmony between the confederate units, keeping possible conflicts away. Every single territory was ruled by a monarch (Oba), the council of monarchs, the leaders of the guilds, and Egbe (the merchants).

In addition, government power was passed down from generation to generation, except in some territories where the appointment of a king on the basis of royal descent had been abolished and open to any male born in the territory. Generally, the Obas were polygamous, and it is said that some of them married a disproportionate number of wives, even over 25. Marriage was one of the main means to increase political power; for this reason, they preferred to marry women of royal lineage.

In the 16th century, the decline of the power of the Yoruba confederacy began, and the peace that had reigned for years was interrupted by the first conflicts. Conflicts with the Sokoto Caliphate of the northern region were the main causes of this decline. The Sokoto Caliphate was an Islamic empire founded by Uthman Dan Fodio, and forcibly took control of a northern Yoruba city, causing riots and riots, resulting in a massive retreat of the besieged population in the southern regions.

A choice that will prove wicked because the swamps and the tsetse fly caused the death of men and horses. The Uthman Dan Fodio intensified the offensive to conquer the remaining territories but was defeated by Ibadan, "the savior of the Yoruba land" in 1840.

Nigeria became a UK protectorate in 1901 and then a colony in 1914.

In the following years, Nigerian nationalism grew greatly, and the United Kingdom led the colony, made up of numerous factions and ethnic groups, towards self-government on a federal basis. Colonization, religiously speaking, marked the beginning of Christianity in Nigeria, which resulted in a gradual decline in traditional Yoruba practices and beliefs.

Nigeria gained independence on October 1, 1960, and the entire Yoruba land was incorporated into present-day Nigeria, which became a republic three years after independence.

Today, the Yoruba people live in Nigeria's three major cities of Lagos, Ibadan, and Abeokuta. The majority of people from this culture are spread throughout West Africa, with significant communities in Los Angeles, Chicago, and New York. The Yoruba people have a rich oral tradition that includes proverbs, sayings, and myths that have been passed down to every generation within the family community.

African culture is an amazing blend of West, Central, South, and various other African influences. Yoruba people are one of the dominant ethnic groups in the country who are known to have an immense cultural influence on present-day Nigeria. They are also one of the largest multicultural ethnic groups within Nigeria, with their population estimated at around 19%, according to 2011 census data. The Yoruba are believed to have originated from Benin, which was also known as Ife. They are one of the groups of people who are called the Igbo by the others, after their kingdom.

Yoruba is a Bantu language, which is far more prominent in Western Nigeria than it is in the North. The Yoruba culture has its roots in Benin, where it flourished for centuries before being influenced by many other cultures.

It is interesting to note that due to the influence of the large ethnic groups that came later, there are differences between northern and southern Yorubas today. Yoruba in the South has a much richer culture than that of their counterparts in the North. They have a more complex system of ritual, which they follow for the religious ceremonies.

Yoruba are extremely religious people. Yoruba people are considered to be one of the most spiritual ethnic groups in the country, with few Yoruba areas being considered ghost towns or abandoned settlements. The Yoruba also pride themselves on being very good-looking people and believe that beauty is important in life. Yoruba women have an intricate social hierarchy that can be traced back to the original "Oyo Midan," where only the senior women were allowed to mix with men outside of their communities. The Yoruba are also made up of many different clans, each with their own unique customs regarding marriage, marriage rituals, and rules.

The Yoruba have a very elaborate wedding ritual. This ritual is believed to have originated from the time when kings were still around. Yoruba people believe that if the process of marriage is not followed to the T, it may bring misfortune upon the couple after they are married. The practice can be traced back to an incident that took place in Ibadan during the colonial period. It was then realized that women who got married to men other than their intended groom would always end up ill or dead after their wedding reception, which many people attributed to witchcraft by the woman's family. The practice of this ritual was then formalized, and it became a part of Yoruba culture.

Yoruba people perform many rites of passage during their lives, such as the "Gbedu." This is where women undergo a ceremony to free themselves from all bad spirits such as those which may cause disease and the like. The Yorubas believe that through this ceremony, they will be protected from bad spirits and can lead happy lives. The Gbedu is offered to an elderly woman who already has two children, is with child, or has been widowed with no children. It is then her duty to take care of her extended family members after that age. The Gbedu is a mock ceremony that is usually held indoors and involves the exchange of gifts, such as money, to the elderly woman's family members.

The Yoruba belief in witchcraft has also been known to be popular among their culture. Witches are believed to cause harm or disease by making use of charms and other items. Sadly, the

Yoruba people believe that these people can cause harm through any means and not just by using charms. The Yoruba still perform many rituals designed to prevent evil spirits from entering their homes and causing harm to their family members.

There are great aspects of Yoruba culture that can be seen today in present society, such as music, dance, and even fashion styles. These have been handed down from generation to generation until they became popular amongst the general population. These aspects of Yoruba culture continue to be popular in present-day society, and most people can still identify with them.

Yoruba culture is very rich and vibrant. It is only right that every Nigerian learns more about their local cultures and traditions to appreciate what they have inherited from their ancestors and how they can be beneficial in their lives today.

Yorubaland is a cultural region in southwestern Nigeria. The term may also be used to refer to the traditional religion of the Yoruba, which originated in southwestern Nigeria (though it has spread into neighboring Benin and Togo).

The Birth of Yoruba Culture in Africa and Its Great Importance

As noted, Yoruba culture is one of the most dominant cultures in Africa and has played a significant role in shaping modern-day Africa. It continues to influence many regions of the world with its vibrant individuality.

There are over 35 million Yorubas living today, but not all know how they got to be where they are now. There have been many theories of the origins of Yoruba culture, with the most common being that it came from Igboland. We now know that this theory is inaccurate because there are many similarities between Igboland and Yoruba.

The first Yoruba were considered to have come from Benin City, which is now part of Nigeria; however, there is evidence that they may have come from what is currently known as the Oyo Empire, which was located in present-day Nigeria.

There are many reasons why most historians agree with this theory. They share similar cultural practices, such as their belief in ancestor worship.

Another theory is that they are the descendants of Nok, or in modern-day political terms, Nupes. They were believed to have come from current-day Cameroon and migrated into the Oyo Empire. It is believed that they were traders who migrated around 500 years ago; however, there is evidence of this earlier on; it is thought that they were already trading long before 500 years ago. This theory also makes sense because they share similar cultural practices, such as their way of dressing and how both groups speak Ewe/Fon (a language belonging to the Kwa family).

The Yoruba were predominantly farmers and hunters. They were also skilled craftsmen who produced pottery, woodwork, bronze, and ironworks.

Yoruba traditional religion is built around the belief in a supreme deity called Olodumare and a pantheon of lesser deities known as the orixas. The orixas represent a natural phenomenon: their appearances can be seen in rivers, forests, mountains, and other manifestations of nature, while the descendants of these gods are humans whose personalities reflect the characteristics of that god.

There are many principles used by Yoruba, such as moderation and balance. Yoruba religion is based on a belief that a divine being created them, and they must do as this being says if they want to be rewarded after death. It was also believed that there were many different gods who ruled the world, and you needed to please each of them if you wanted to be rewarded after death.

Yoruba people believe in the saying "Aje bi o ji o ti," which means

"A person with a good heart will always have a good eye." This means that a person with a good heart will always see good, which can be believed by looking at how lovely their towns are. They believe that things should not only look beautiful, but they should be beautiful as well.

As an African society, the Yoruba came to African American culture through such vital elements as its music. African American music has been influenced by many different elements, including the original Africans. However, most of these elements have been taken from the Yoruba culture.

Origin of the Name "Yoruba"

The Yoruba are referred to as Yoruba by their neighbors because, apparently, they are identified by the way they talk. According to Olawoyin, the Yoruba are called "Ogho-Ojo," which means "those who go down for water." The name gradually changed to Oyo-Oro because the river Oyo is just below where they live, within their territory.

According to Douglas Johnson in his book "African Traditions," the word "Yoruba" may have come from a strange phenomenon that happened when Europeans first met with the region's people. When the Europeans asked them where they were from, they replied, "O rúba," which means "O the well-rooted trees." The Europeans thought they were saying "O rúba," which is Yoruba. From there, it was reduced to Yoruba.

Another theory of the name "Yoruba" is that it came from the Yoruban word "Orun," which means "to make a sudden movement." This may have referred to the fact that when strangers met with them, they were very abrupt and quick in their movements. However, none of these theories have been proven to be right.

In early history, many African peoples journeyed from one part of Africa to another in search of a place they could call their own.

This was a hard task for people looking for a home because they had to travel through miles and miles of desert and jungles with little food or water in order to reach their destination alive.

The Yoruba were one of the many African migrants who traveled east in search of a place to call home. They migrated out of their territory, the Oyo Empire, and reached what is now modern-day Benin, Togo, and Cameroon. They came upon what they believed to be a potential home that was located on two rivers known as the Niger and the Benue. This was where they thought they would find fertile land for their crops.

The Yoruba were not considered to be very politically active until Olowo Ajulo became Ooni of Ife in 1809. This made him one of the most important leaders in Yorubaland for nearly 50 years until he died in 1854 at age 78. He was the first Yoruba Ooni to succeed his father, Oba Abasanjo, who was Ooni of Ife at the same time.

After his death, Oba Ajao Adeoyo I took over as the traditional authority of Yorubaland. He had little power because he was not considered to be very strong-willed or trusted by the people. His son, Oba Osinlade Ogodo, became Ooni of Ife shortly after his father's death in 1864. He held this position until he died in 1885 at age 65.

History of the Yoruba People

There are several stories that describe the Yoruba people. The most popular of these stories was the story of their origin, which they refer to as "Okolikaji."

The Yoruba were a tribe who lived in a small region in present-day Nigeria, which they called Ife. They were a thriving and successful city-state closely tied with its larger neighbors, Igboland and Benin. Their society was very advanced and was one of the most successfully organized civilizations in Africa at the time.

By the mid-1970s, nearly half of all Nigerian citizens lived in Ife, making it the most densely populated place on earth at that time.

They were known for their impressive art, high level of trade, and incredibly advanced methods of building. At the peak of their success as a civilization, many other cultures tried to imitate them, which is why there are so many Yoruba-influenced cities today. Although they no longer exist as a single culture since they were conquered by other people or assimilated into different cultures, there still remain large numbers of Yoruba people and territories that carry on the culture and traditions of the first Yoruba peoples.

As mentioned above, The first Yoruba were considered to have come from Benin city, which is now part of Nigeria. However, there is evidence that they may have come from what is currently known as the Oyo Empire. While there are similarities between the Igboland and Yoruba, it has been concluded that the Yoruba integration into Igboland was much later than their neighboring regions. The people who migrated into Igboland were said to be fleeing the Fulani Jihad of 1804 and 1805.

While it is believed by many historians that these people came over from Benin City, it has also been said that some did migrate from Oyo and Ife at around this time. Despite this, most believe that the Yoruba were not a centralized society at this time, and they spent most of their time in their separate city-states.

However, even though the Yorubas were separated by their respective city-states, they still had very close ties with one another. They shared many beliefs and practiced many similar rituals. Of course, just like any other society in history, there were always conflicts between one another, and no matter how strong the relationship between neighboring states was, they could never stay together indefinitely.

Expansion to Other Parts of the World

What is the Yoruba religion? The answer cannot be unambiguous. First of all, it is the religion of the Orisha, which arrived with the diaspora of slaves in Brazil and Cuba and spread massively after 1950, but it is also the Pentecostalism of many Nigerians who have emigrated in recent decades to European countries and those of Sub-Saharan Africa, especially to large cities like Nairobi and Johannesburg. Not only that but at the same time, there are Yoruba in Africa. Some of whom, albeit with difficulty and compromise, continue to practice the "old religion," along with various forms of Islam and Christianity that those practices demonize.

For the sake of clarity, let us distinguish "three concentric circles" of Yoruba religion, which are, from the innermost to the outermost:

1) The religion practiced by the Yoruba in their homeland, which is conventionally called "Yoruba traditional religion" (YTR) and which has at its core the worship of the Orisha;

1) The religion followed by the vast majority of Yoruba today, consisting of various forms of Islam and Christianity (neo-Pentecostalism and other evangelical offshoots), oriented towards a general anti-Orisha sentiment;

2) The Yoruba religion is practiced outside Nigeria in various parts of the world by people who are not Yoruba or their descendants.

Between the first and third circles, there is an intimate connection and, at the same time, a continuous contradiction. The cult of the Orisha has had not only lasting, but a growing impulse and flowering outside Africa. Whereas, at home, these supernatural entities only dimly retain the importance they had in tribal cults before the dominant Christian and Muslim groups made them the object of theological attacks by declaring them "demonic."

At the base of the traditional Yoruba religion, in its two directions inside and outside Nigeria, is the YTR. First of all, the term "Yoruba" itself, of Arab origin, was used to designate only the Oyo, one of the most important of the many ethnic groups that populated the region. Adopted by the Anglican missionary Church in 1840, the name was extended to all the local populations that it was intended to evangelize, similar in language and culture, and, above all, who considered themselves descendants of Ife-Ife.

However, these diverse groups found greater unity in the context of slavery in the Americas, where they also often had to defend themselves against other very different African ethnic groups such as the Lucumi in Cuba, the Nago in Brazil, and the Aku in Sierra Leone. What, more than all the different origins or affiliations, counts in the "Yoruba" identification is the devotion to the Orisha, which can manifest itself in Nigeria in an extreme variety of local forms different from city to city. For example, Shangò, who plays a predominant role in the South American cult, was an Oyo deity practically ignored by the eastern ethnic groups; Oduduwa was an ancestral (male) commander of Ife in the central-eastern regions while she is considered the (female) consort of the god of creation in the southwest; among river deities, Yemoja belonged mainly to the west, Osun to the center and east while Oya, connected to the Niger River and tornadoes, to the north. Geographical location favored the western regions, home to the preeminent Oyo. Islam had arrived over the more remote east and its inaccessible forests.

The flow of Yoruba slaves to the Americas was continuous and massive. Especially between the 1810s and 1826-50, a period when the social and political weakening of the Oyo left a power vacuum and decades of internecine wars, until well after the abolition of slavery by France and Britain in the 1930s as human trafficking continued through illegal routes to the Spanish and Portuguese colonies, where slavery was later abolished (in Cuba in 1886, in Brazil in 1888). The ability of these cults to survive adversity and change while maintaining a strong African

connotation is, therefore, due to their adaptability, but also to a series of other circumstances: for example, in the colonies of Latin America, Catholic missionaries and evangelicals were better prepared than their Protestant and Anglican counterparts to recognize and accept the existence of different African nations and allow them to associate in a limited sphere of activity, a condition that understandably favored the survival of the traditions; the cabildos, missionary institutions, had this aggregative function and, at the same time, provided an important framework within which to maintain the cult of the Orisha in the process of syncretic dissimulation with Catholic saints and their Iberian-Baroque iconography.

Therefore, the necessity of adaptation and new inspirations have led to a reduction in the number of deities present in indefinite quantity in the traditional religion. The primary "survivors" (Sango, Ogun, Yemoja, Esu-Elegba, Obatala, Ososi, Osun, Oya, Sopona, or Babaluaye) have in common that they come from the central and north-western regions of Yorubaland. In particular, Sango, a royal god for the Oyo and who also assumed a prominent position in America to the point of eclipsing even, in some cases, the importance of the others (think of the Brazilian Xango or the Shango of Trinidad). Other Orisha has disappeared in certain regions and flourished in others - Orunmila, for example, is almost non-existent in Brazil, while in Cuba, it is the object of great devotion.

The complex rituals of Yoruba derivation then developed a modern, rational theological and ritual organization in response to the impact of a non-African context and its tools as a resource. This transformation of the religion of the Orisha into a true belief system involved a sort of "pantheonization" of the cult under the banner of unification and hierarchy, similar to what is found in Greco-Roman religion. Still, it is a slippery road to travel, an abstraction, when the concrete reality consists of many different cults in various. Unlike in the New World colonies, the Orisha have never shared festivals or temples. Indeed, their relations are marked by open rivalry.

Hence the religion of the Orisha in the Americas seems to take two different paths; the first marked by African Americans and the other, in particular, by the Santeros of Cuba, wherein the late nineteenth century five Yoruba Babalawo established the Regla de Ifa and founded its main branches.

The "third circle" (expansion of the religion of Orisha outside Africa) includes two different lines of historical development: that of the contraction, in Nigeria, of the cult of the Orisha and the opposite and contrary line of expansion in the radically new context of the diaspora. These two directions produced, on the one hand, the desire of Yoruba African Americans for a "return to Africa," revisionism that would provide answers to the need for ethnic integrity, and, on the other, the Yorubización, an inclusive opening supported above all by the Cubans, who had introduced the religion of the Orisha into the United States at the end of the 1940s. Afro-Cuban religions are characterized by a "theology of non-racially marked recruitment" because, in Cuba, these cults did not identify with blackness, as on the contrary happened in the United States.

The most concrete result of the first current was the founding of a village in South Carolina called Oyotunji (Oyo Revived), still active and operating today. In this place, a Yoruba community has literally reinvented itself, respecting a cycle of ceremonies dedicated to the major Orisha and appealing to divination to learn about its African ancestors. Its founder, the Oba Adefunmi (Walter S. King by birth), first lived through a more eclectic phase, today one would say "open to contamination" (especially from the Aka and Dahomei) until, towards the end of the 1950s, he formed a special bond with a Santero, Cristóbal Oliana, and then turned sharply towards the political positions of black nationalism. The result on the religious level was, on the one hand, the refusal to accept that non-black people could be initiated into the traditional religion, and on the other hand, the need for legitimacy coming directly from the Oni of Ife, the highest authority on the matter. According to this orientation, the "primordial" rituals and doctrinal formulas, coming from Ife-Ife as the place of cosmogony, have greater effectiveness. But African Americans on this side of the Atlantic did not suspect that, paradoxically, this charge is, if not a Christian subject, at least strongly influenced by the Pentecostal presence of the dominant community; and that for their part, Nigerians consider the "new" Yoruba of Adefunmi as Yojimbo ("Europeans," no more than outsiders).

In Nigeria, Islam and Christianity are the foreign and hegemonic religions with respect to the indigenous population, which suffers their influences: the Church of Orunmila, for example, founded in the 1920s, models its services on those of the Protestant churches, with the result that is anything but primitive and original. But on the fortunate wings of this need for recognition flew many episcopal advantages, ceremonial experts and Babalawo, the best known of whom was Professor Wande Abimbola, Ifa's spokesman in the world on behalf of the Ooni himself, whose task is to promote Nigerian Yoruba practice as "normative" and who has found greater support in Brazil than in Cuba, where the Regla de Ifa prevails.

The profound decline of traditional religion in Yorubaland corresponds, in America, the search for the original wisdom to which to refer and by which to feel legitimized, becoming the means for a tradition that one would like to be uninterrupted. Spurious elements are expunged in respect of a re-Africanization that becomes a sort of "desyncretization," in sharp contrast with the accommodating and dogma-free nature of the religion of the Orisha, that ability to mix-and-match with the variegated forms of African Protestantism, with the even more aerial new age spirituality or with other non-Yoruba African traditions capable of creating syncretic products continually distinguished by the freshness of contemporaneity.

It must be admitted that the Yoruba are no longer the primary vectors of their traditional religion, but Afro-Caribbeans and African-Americans are no less so now than devout Latinos.

Santeria and Candomblé are the classic examples of a good result in adapting flexibly to the point of losing any obligation with the ethnolinguistic provenance. This is the first requirement for the Orisha to aspire to become a World religion of the third millennium.

THE YORUBA RELIGION

What is Yoruba?

Yoruba is a religion practiced by over 50 million people--the plurality religion in Nigeria, Benin, Togo, and Ghana. It's also practiced in Trinidad and Tobago, Cuba, Dominican Republic, and Suriname.

As already described in the previous chapters, the Yoruba religion is named after a group of people living in southwestern Nigeria. That's why people also call it "Ori-Igbon," which means "the religion of the Yoruba people."

The Yoruba religion is sometimes called Lucumi or Santeria, but those names aren't as accurate as Yoruba. In fact, they're Spanish words that mean "light" and "sanctuary." When they were first used in Cuba as a name for the Yoruba religion, Lucumi and Santeria were used to describe all African religions.

The Yoruba Religion is NOT Santeria. There are some similarities between them, but there are also many significant differences.

Yoruba is derived from the Yoruba people who live in southwestern Nigeria. They are ethnically diverse but have some commonalities in terms of their history, culture, language, and mythology. So the Yoruba religion really has little to do with Cuba or Santeria.

Santeria is derived from the word "santaria." Santaria is a word for religion in several African languages, including Yoruba. It's important to clarify this because the Yoruba religion is sometimes confused with Santeria or Lucumi. If that happens, it's not accurate. A better description of the Yoruba religion would be "Yorubaland African Traditional Religion" or "Yoruba African Traditional Religion." That's because the Yoruba are only one African ethnic group among many that practice similar religions. Cuba is the only country where the Yoruba religion has been called "Santeria" or "Lucumi." In other parts of the world, it's more commonly known as "Yoruba."

The Yoruba religion is a very old religion with a rich mythology and a complex pantheon of deities. It's an important part of African Traditional Religion, which includes a number of similar religions practiced throughout Africa, the Caribbean, and South America.

The Yoruba religion is derived from the Yoruba people who live in southwestern Nigeria.

That's why it's sometimes called "Ori-Igbon," which means "the religion of the Yoruba people." While "Yoruba" and "Ori-Igbon" both mean the same thing, Ori-Igbon is more accurate because it uses the group's name that practices this religion.

It spread through much of the African Diaspora, including Cuba, Brazil, Trinidad, and Venezuela. It's also practiced in Benin, Togo, Ghana, the Bahamas. The Yoruba religion has many similarities with other African indigenous religions.

The Yoruba people are ethnically diverse and have commonalities in terms of their history, culture, language, and mythology. They regard themselves as original human beings. Many of them believe that they were formed from the union of Orishala and Oduduwa.

The Yoruba religion is often confused with Santeria, also called "Lucumi." This confusion stems from the fact that these two religions have many similarities. For example, there are Yoruba people in Cuba and Lucumi/Santeria priests in Nigeria. Cuba and Nigeria were the first nations to be colonized by Spain and Portugal, respectively. This means that Spanish Catholicism influenced many Lucumi/Santeria priests. The Yoruba religion is usually not influenced by Catholicism.

There are some differences between Lucumi (Santeria) and the Yoruba religion, such as:

The most important difference is that Lucumi (Santeria) is a syncretic religion, while the Yoruba religion is not. Lucumi (Santeria) has incorporated many Catholic elements into its practices. The Yoruba religion is not syncretic. It has kept its African roots intact.

Many people practice both the traditional Yoruba religion and Christianity because of the influence of colonialism on African societies. These individuals are not practicing syncretism but rather are practicing both religions side-by-side. They simply choose to worship one deity on Sunday and another on Tuesday. This is also true for those who practice Lucumi (Santeria) and the Yoruba religion. Many people in Cuba, Trinidad, and Venezuela practice both religions.

The Yoruba religion is not a new religion. It's very old and has been passed down from generation to generation orally. It uses a number of orishas, which are spirits that have been recognized by the Yoruba people since time immemorial. They respond to prayers called "Ifá," "Oshun," and "Olorun," among others. These are spirits of nature, wisdom, divination, and communications. Some of them also embody deities that came to the Yoruba people through trade with other cultures. For example, the orisha of "Ogun" may have originated in Nigeria or Benin.

The Yoruba religion is not just an African religion. It's also referred to as Obeah because it was introduced by Angolan slaves into the Caribbean. This religion was brought to the Caribbean by Yorubas, who were brought over during the slave trade. They sold their skills as blacksmiths and other occupations and also sold their beliefs in African deities. In fact, both Lucumi/Santeria and Obeah have been associated with witchcraft.

There are also similarities between the Yoruba religion and Candomblé, which is practiced in Brazil. Candomblé originated from the Yoruba religion, but it has been influenced by Catholicism and indigenous Brazilian spirituality. Brazil's history with the slave trade is similar to Cuba's history. In fact, many slaves who were brought to Cuba came from Brazil. This means that Yoruba people were brought to Cuba and that the Yoruba religion was brought to Brazil. The same is true for Haiti and Trinidad, which also experienced a significant influx of Yoruba slaves. The Yoruba religion has been practiced in those countries as well.

There are also similarities between the Yoruba religion and Vodou, which is practiced in Haiti. Many of the Yoruba deities have been incorporated into Vodou rituals.

The Yoruba religion does not have a priesthood. Vodou priests, for example, are a respected group who take on the role of godfathers and godmothers of children and offer aid to those who seek their aid. The Vodou priesthood is not hereditary. Anyone can serve the gods of the Yoruba religion, whether they are male or female. There are no houses of priests in the Yoruba religion. Almost all Yoruba people who practice this religion are part of a lineage that is associated with a god or goddess, but they do not refer to themselves as priests. In fact, there is no word in the Yoruba language for a priest. This is because the Yoruba religion has no priesthood. Though, there are spiritual leaders that can be associated with the title priest or priestess.

The Yoruba religion does not have the concept of a temple. The Yoruba people do not build temples and other buildings that would be dedicated to a god or goddess. There are, however, shrines, which are places where important events occur in Yoruba life. These include birth, marriage, and death, as well as other celebrations such as rites of passage and funerals.

The Yoruba religion uses an abidjan (kwassa k'osin) to perform divination. It is made of palm fibers and is steeped in the oil of the sacred plant, "kelewele" (banana tree). It is considered to be a gift from the gods. Sorcery (which is often referred to as Ifá or "Oshun") can also be performed with this Abidjan.

What Do Yoruba People Believe?

One of the most important concepts in the Yoruba religion is the figure of "Olorun."

"Olorun" means "lord" or "owner of paradise."

He is the supreme deity and creator of the Yoruba African people.

An important key to the Yoruba religion, to live in peace and to be good followers, is to follow the Orishas.

"Orishas" are spirits. They are the most important deities in the Yoruba religion. Orisa means "head" in the Yoruba language, which refers to each Orishas presiding over a different part of people's lives. The head is considered the most important part of the human body, so it makes sense that Orishas would preside over different aspects of life.

Each Orisha has certain characteristics, which are often represented through animals. For example, Oya is believed to have braided hair, so she's worshiped with a comb.

Each Orisha has the power to control the things around her. They are also believed to interact with people in ways that affect their lives. For example, Babalu Aye is said to be able to increase the size of people's bodies, and Eleda is known as the goddess of marriage (among other things).

These deities are worshiped by the Yoruba and almost all Africans who practice Traditional Religion. The Orishas are considered essential to daily life and the fulfillment of one's destiny.

Some of the most well-known Orishas include:

Eshu: Eshu is an Orisha of crossroads and boundaries. He's often associated with business and trade, and he has an important role in deciding destinies and making things happen in people's lives.

Odùduwà: Odùduwà is the Orisha recognized as the father of the Yoruba people.

Obatala: Obatala is a principle Orisha in Yorubaland. He's also the Orisha of creation and the ruler of heaven. People who don't follow any other Orisha often follow him instead. Some people consider him a principle Orisha in African Traditional Religion.

Ogun: Ogun is a main orisha warrior and hunter known for his skill with a blade. A demigod of war, fire, iron, hunting, and agriculture, he is considered both a creator and a destroyer, protector of blacksmiths and metalworkers, soldiers, and mechanics.

Oya: Oya is the goddess of storms. She is often worshiped with drumming and dancing, which attracts her attention, so she will cause destruction. People also worship Eleda for marriage and Obatala for children, but they also pray to Oya for protection during storms.

Oshun: Oshun is the goddess of beauty, sexuality, and love. She is worshipped for marriage, children, beauty, and fertility.

Oshumare: Osumare has the meaning of rainbow in the Yoruba language. In fact, it is considered the spirit of the rainbow.

Ọba ': Oba' is the female Orisha of the Oba River and is identified as Shango's elderly wife.

Oshosi: Oshosi is a god of nature who is worshiped for the bounty of the land. He's often indirectly associated with good harvests, so farmers and hunters worship him for protection from wild animals.

Shango: Shango is a warrior-king who overthrew his brother and established a new government. Some people worship him as the equivalent of Zeus in Greek mythology, while others consider him a principle Orisha in African Traditional Religion. He's considered a war god because, as a warrior-king, he was the one who won the Yoruba people freedom from bondage and oppression. His festival celebrated his victory over his brother, so it's also known as a "freedom festival."

Shango is also worshipped for success in business and for good fortunes. Shango is by far the most popular deity among Yoruba people for business or financial success

Olokun: Olokun was originally a hero, later became Orisha. He is the one who governs mental health, material wealth, dreams, and psychic abilities. He is a divinity linked to the sea.

Yemoja: Yemoja is considered the queen of the sea and controls the waters. She is a protective mother but also has a destructive aspect, symbolized by the stormy sea. She is the eldest daughter of Olokun.

Fundamental Beliefs And Traditions In The Yoruba

The Five Fundamental Beliefs That Make Up the Yoruba:

Firstly, and most importantly, your god and goddess is the god and goddess of your ancestors. Your Orishas are supposed to be manifestations of them. Your ancestors died so that you could live.

Secondly, the Yoruba believe that death is an integral part of life. Before they can take their place in the afterlife, people must die to free up their energy to move into the spirit world. This is called "reaping." Reaping is involuntary, so people who are still living are unable to participate. When someone dies, they are thought to leave the material world forever.

Thirdly, it's important for West Africans to keep their ancestors alive through rituals and ceremonies to provide them with love and protection. The Yoruba believe that the dead are afraid of being forgotten. If they aren't remembered by their families or friends after they die, they become restless and worried about being forgotten in the afterlife. They stay in the world of the dead, and they become disrupted and unhappy. If they aren't remembered, then their souls cannot continue into the material world. Consequently, people who forget their ancestors or don't keep them alive through ceremonies or rituals suffer because their bodies aren't properly aligned with the material world, and so they can also be disruptive.

Fourthly, West Africans believe that everyone has a personal god and goddess called your Orishas. Orishas are the Yoruba's manifestation of the gods, goddesses, and spirits that they believe exist in the spirit world. Your Orishas can be either male or female. They each have their own attributes and characteristics, just like every other god in the material world. Every person has their own Orishas, so people in the Yoruba belief system are often surprised when they visit another person in West Africa and see that person's Orishas in their possession. Fifthly, the Yoruba believe that everyone has a spirit guardian, a deity that protects them from harm and misfortune.

The Yoruba religion provides a full-scale system for guiding people through their lives. Every aspect of someone's life, from birth to death, is thought to be under the control of one or more Orishas. Therefore, the Yoruba believe that if you do something considered disloyal to your Orishas, they will be angry with you. They will become upset because their relationship with you has been damaged or broken. This can result in negative things happening to you or your family, like sickness or death.

To avoid making the Orishas unhappy, people participate in many rituals and ceremonies throughout the year.

Traditions of the Yoruba People

Naming of children

-The Yoruba people believe that naming someone is an act of respect. Because they are the ones who will be providing the child with physical existence, they must be respected. So, if there's a possibility that you might want to change their name, later on, it would be best to think about them carefully before calling them by another name.

-There is a belief in the Yoruba culture that the children of people who die young are more fortunate than those who live long lives.

Marriage

-For the Yoruba people, weddings are very special events. When a couple gets married, they are considered to have joined one another in a relationship that goes beyond the material world. Therefore, they are no longer considered separate entities; rather, they become one in the relationship between two people.

-There is also an idea in their culture that marriages should be special occasions when there is great joy mixed with sadness because separation is inevitable when two people join together in marriage.

Importance of deceased relatives

-When a person dies, they are supposed to be remembered and honored by the living. However, unlike other belief systems, the Yoruba believe that it is not enough for them to simply remember their deceased family and friends. They also believe that they must continue to provide them with love and material goods in the form of food and clothing until they get to the next world.

OLODUMARE/OLORUN

Olodumare/Olorun is the highest deity in the Yoruba religion and is sometimes called Olode. It is believed that he created the earth and heavens and resides at their highest point, often considered to be a transcendent location. He is the king of the gods, and in some stories, Olorun creates all. He does not have children.

According to the Yoruba, Olorun is the force of all life force. He is considered to be an omnipotent being who embodies the power of the universe. He is said to have created everything in existence by giving it form, including people. It also means "light", "brightness", or "light-beam" in Ijebuano language. Olorun is the personification of the heavens.

In some cultures, Yoruba people worship Olodumare as a monotheistic God, while some others worship him as a plurality of gods. When he first created the earth from water and soil, Olorun gave control to lesser gods. As a result, some believe that he has no control over human lives on earth and is unable to affect them directly. Olorun is associated with the elements such as water and earth.

In the traditional Yoruba religion, Olorun is seen as a supreme deity who is above all others, including Oduduwa (also known as

Oludumare and Yemoja) and Oduduwa's son Shango (called Eshin or Sango). Orisha Ogun (also known as Oni) and Osa (also known as Oro) are also worshiped by some Yoruba people. Oduduwa is a creator or fashioner of all things, including the Earth and sky. Ogun is the divinity of fire, weapons, and iron.

In Yoruba cosmology, several pairs of deities carry out various functions in the world. In some stories, Olorun is considered mortal or semi-mortal due to his ability to make mistakes. His mistakes are often attributed to being the cause of humanity's challenges during its evolution on earth. When the world was first created, his mistakes gave rise to the people who were also made from clay.

Other Orishas are often considered as his children, such as Yewa (also known as Oshun), Oya, and Osun. Other deities include Ade (also known as Olodumare) and Shango (also known as Eshu).

In the Yoruba religion, Ogun is a malevolent deity of war and iron, and he is one of the most important deities in Yoruba culture. This deity is popular among the Yoruba people and is mentioned frequently in their folklore.

Ogun was not originally a god in the Yoruba pantheon but became significant because of his association with warfare and blacksmiths. It might also be the same god as Oni, a name sometimes applied to Ogun. In addition to weapons and war, Ogun is a deity associated with agriculture, politics, hunting, and blacksmiths, among other things.

Olodumare is also one of the most important deities in Santeria, a system of faiths originating with the Yoruba slaves who were transported from Nigeria to Cuba, Puerto Rico, and other Caribbean islands. In Santeria, he is known as Olorun and called "The Creator." Olorun is mentioned in the prayers of a priest or a "filhos" (child) in Santeria.

Prayers are said to him so that he may help humanity. As the Supreme Creator of the world, Olorun is associated with peace, harmony, justice, fairness, and equity. He also takes an interest in humanity's well-being. When people are suffering on Earth due to crime or injustice, it is believed that Olorun is disturbed as well. He is approached through prayer or offerings at a shrine dedicated to him.

Olodumare is the supreme god of the Yoruba religion in that he is believed to be older than all other deities or non-deities. However, this is not necessarily true. He was created when the world was made before humans existed, but he did not create humans. It was Olorun who gave humanity life on Earth.

As the creator of the world, Olodumare is credited with all creation. If a baby is born to a family, then he or she is believed to be a creation of Olorun. He sees everything and knows everything that happens on earth. It is believed that the mistakes humans make are due to him communicating with them directly. He only speaks to the people on earth through oracles.

Once, Olodumare sent a messenger to earth to tell humans that they would receive divine resurrection if they lived well on earth. When this message was brought back, Olodumare was pleased with humanity's reaction and decided to give them immortality and rule over the world (Bashorun and Ajayi, 2012).

Olodumare is said to be invisible and all-knowing. Because of his great knowledge, it is said that he is able to see everything. His only eyes are the eyes of the people.

Since he is invisible, people can see him through dreams and visions. In this vision, they will often see Olodumare in red. People also see him as a white or pink-haired old man who wears a crown on his head and a black cloth around his waist (Arinze, 2005).

Some call him the "spirit of love" because he is believed to be the people's teacher. He gives very wise teachings to people. If someone does not act in accordance with his teachings, he will punish them by causing them to fall ill or to die (Ajayi, 2005).

The purpose of Olodumare is two-fold: First, he tries to help humans survive on earth and teach them how to survive it. Second, he makes them know what he wants of them. He also helps the people of the earth when they are in trouble.

Originally, Olodumare was a river divinity that emerged from the Ogun River and branched into several streams. He was called "the one who is unlimited." In time, this river divinity became known as the highest of all gods.

In Yewa, where he came from, he had a female counterpart called Olokun. She was conceived of as his consort, the feminine part of the Supreme Being. She was considered the mother-creatress of all things

Olodumare created several deities in Yoruba mythology. Among them are Ogun, the god of iron; Agbada (also known as Ogboni), god of irrigation; Oya, goddess of thunder; Okanran, god of war; Ibinabo, land goddess; Oduduwa, god of lightning; Obatala, supreme God who was originally thought to be Olodumare.

Oya, the mother of the gods, was said to be Olodumare's daughter. She had her own children, Kanu and Kunu. She was also the wife of Orisha-nla.

As in most myths, all children of Olodumare grew up to be gods. Orunla, the god of divination; Ana, the god of wine; and Aganju, the god of thunder and war, were among these (Arinze, 2005).

Another deity created by Olodumare was Erinle. He is sometimes referred to as Eshu-Alafin (Eshu is the divine messenger in Yoruba religion). He later became the messenger of Olodumare.

Olodumare is often identified with or called "Olorun," which means something like "the all-knowing and all-powerful." Olorun is synonymous with the Roman god Jupiter: both gods had a connection with light and were considered ruling deities in some parts of Africa (Watkins 2004).

As the supreme deity, Olorun's primary roles are that of creative energy and spiritual leader. He is responsible for providing an area of protected space, referred to as "Olorun's realm," within which to conduct spiritual, religious, or family activities. This realm is envisioned as a place where heaven and earth meet through clouds or water waves. He also furnishes the people with the material resources needed for sustenance and survival (Ajayi 2005).

As the supreme deity, Olodumare is associated with "Elusi" or "Iroru," which are aspects of deities that are observed in their creation, often directly by Olodumare ("Orun" in Yoruba) through dreams. These particular deities are said to be the most powerful of all but still fall under the orders of Olorun. Their role is to protect human beings from harm or evil spirits. It is believed that their presence will strengthen people. They are important to the people because they provide protection (Ajayi, 2005).

Relatives and ancestors can also protect an individual. Olorun protects and watches over everyone, but other spirits and deities may help as well.

The Orishas (Deities) were created by Olorun after he created humanity. He ordered them to create humans as well as teach them how to survive on earth (Ajayi, 2005). The Orishas became angry at Olorun because they were unhappy with their creations. They told Olorun that they wanted to make their own creations (humanity) and not be ordered about and also teach the humans. Olodumare agreed. The Orishas were assigned different tasks, such as rain, agriculture, water, fire, and other natural phenomena, which often involved sending messages to humans through oracles (Arinze 2005).

Since Olodumare created everything on earth, he is thought to be the guardian of life. When someone dies, he is also responsible for giving them a new body.

The worship of Olodumare has declined over the years due to Oyo Empire's conversion to Islam, but some still hold on to the faith. There are many celebrations of Olodumare's birthday in Yorubaland. In the state of Oyo state, Olodumare is called

"Ebereyi" or "Ebusun" and is worshiped through numerous shrines all over the state. In Ibadan, one of the largest cities in Nigeria, Olodumare is worshiped at a large shrine known as the "Amenle" or "Agbado." In Nigeria, he is also known as Obi Nla (Obiasun). Some people may choose to call him by his Yoruba name.

Olodumare's main celebrations are held at the beginning of the year, usually during the first two weeks of December. The festivals are mainly held inside shrines to honor Olodumare.

Aside from being celebrated through festivals, Olodumare is also worshiped in many other ways. There are many shrines dedicated to him for people who may not be able to go to the festivals. Amulets and pieces of cloth with his image cut out on them are also worn by followers. This is done to remind them to always follow Olodumare's teachings, such as sacrifice and selflessness (Ajayi 2005).

Human beings are not the only things that Olodumare creates. He has also created plants, animals, and objects such as the crossbow and the human body. He is thought to hold a relationship with all creation in Yorubaland.

In Yorubaland, the crossbow was traditionally used in hunting. It is a device that launches a projectile by means of a mechanism. Olodumare created the crossbow to use for hunting and food gathering. Olodumare taught people how to make the crossbow and warned them against giving it to strangers. He warned that if they disobeyed him, then he would be forced to destroy it. He gave the crossbow to a man, who then shared it with strangers. It was destroyed as promised.

In Yorubaland, the human body is thought to be superior to all other objects created by Olodumare. He created it as a gift for humans to use for over one hundred years. He gave the body many senses and capabilities to make people's lives better. When a person dies, they are given a new body in heaven.

Olodumare is the supreme deity in Yorubaland and has many worshippers. People all around Yorubaland worship him, but there are several annual festivals that are held to celebrate him. Some of these festivals are held on fixed dates, while some are based on lunar calendars. A few of the celebrations include Oba-Ara, Eyo-Owa, Egungun Festivals, Oduduwa Festival and Erin Osa.

Oba-Ara Festival: It is held in Ilesha, Osun State. It is celebrated in March or April. The festival celebrates the Oba of Ilesha, who was also a priest of Olodumare.

Eyo-Owa Celebration: It is held on varying dates every year. There are different celebrations for different villages of Yorubaland, but many celebrate the same festival within the first two weeks of December. The festival is held to celebrate the death anniversary of Oba Ewuare the Great, who was the founder of the Oyo Empire. He was also a priest of Olodumare.

Egungun Festival: It is celebrated in Lagos and Ibadan, Yorubaland. The celebration attracts thousands of people and takes place on the first of January. The festival is believed to commemorate the landing of Oduduwa of Ife on land after he arrived from across the sea (Okafor 1999).

Erin Osa Festival: It takes place on the third of January, in Ibadan. It is celebrated in honor of Erin Osa or Olorun-Ebere, Olodumare's sister. The celebration is held to celebrate the birthday of Olodumare.

Ozo-Oya Celebration: It takes place in Ilesha, Osun State. The celebration is held on the eighth of March or April to celebrate the birth anniversary of Oba Ewuare the Great. He is believed to be the incarnation of Olodumare.

Oduduwa Festival: It is celebrated in Ilesha, Osun State. It signifies the birth of Oduduwa, who was the founder of Ife or Oyo Empire. He was also a priest of Olodumare. This festival takes place on the first week of December every year to celebrate the birth anniversary of Oduduwa.

Ekeremi Festival: It is celebrated in Ibadan, Yorubaland. The festival takes place on the thirteenth of January. It is celebrated to celebrate the birthday of Olorun-Ebere, Olodumare's sister.

Ameko-obi Festival: It takes place in Ibadan, Yorubaland. It is celebrated to celebrate the birthday of Ameko-Ogbon, Olodumare's son and the leader of the Yoruba pantheon.

Iru Festival: It takes place in Ibadan, Yorubaland. It celebrates the birth anniversary of Eshu-Iru, another son of Olodumare and a warrior who fought against human beings.

Festivals such as these are celebrated throughout Yorubaland and many other parts of Nigeria. They are celebrated to honor different deities. Olodumare is the deity of choice for many Yoruba people, and the celebration of his festivals is widespread.

The mythology and rites of passage in Yorubaland take place during one's initiation to adulthood. Many tribes have unique initiation rituals that take place during adolescence, calling it the "Oduduwa Festival." The Yoruba people believe that at birth, a person receives a set period of time before they can be considered an adult.

Initiation rites usually begin at the onset of puberty, which is around 13–15 years old. The Yoruba believe that at this age, one has reached complete physical maturity, and their body is ready to serve their deities. Although it varies by tribe, the initiation rituals are still unique to each culture (Ajayi 2005).

Yoruban mythology states that there are five realms of existence: one material, three spiritual, and an underworld. These realms are divided into four quadrants which together form a cross. The five realms are the upper world, the underworld, the earth, the sea, and the sky. The four quadrants are also known as "odu" (east), "orisa" (south), "ilu" (west), and "oro" (north) odu or orisa ilu Ororo Oduduwa meaning respectively Divine Ancestors and Deities of Creation; Earthly Sacrificial Altars; Sources of Wealth and Power; and Spiritual Forces that maintain order in the universe. In Yoruba cosmology, the sun, moon, and stars are all located in the upper world, which is located in the east. The moon is located in the north and west directions. This cosmology, much like any other creation mythology, works with a hierarchy of creation. For example, the world was originated from a small plant. The divine ancestors were all created by Olodumare as part of Olodumare's plan to create life on earth; hence they are all Olodumare's offspring. They are gods or spirits that live in heaven. Collectively, their name means 'The Ancestors', while individually, they are called Eyo, Oduduwa, Oludumare, etc. They are responsible for bringing life to the world, which is how they came to be known as the ancestral deities.

The qualities of Olodumare

To approach and connect with this important and fundamental figure in the Yoruba religion, it is necessary to understand the characteristics and qualities of Olodumare.

He is the first and **_supreme creator_** of the earth and the universe and also of important figures in the Yoruba religion, the Orishas.

This statement is echoed in one of the stories of the creation of the Yoruba world: at first, the land was inhospitable and swampy, and Olodumare and the Orishas lived in the sky but assiduously visited the land to profess their divine abilities and for hunting.

Wishing to restore the land and have a healthy, non-swampy territory, Olodumare asked Obatala for help in achieving his intention.

Obatala received from Olodumare, a hen, a pigeon, and a snail shell filled with sand, and through the divine chain headed for the land. He started to throw the sand on the ground, and the hen spread it with her feet. Olodumare sent a chameleon to check the work done after receiving the news from the pigeon sent by Obatala.

The next step was to cover the earth with the nuts of the divine palms, which in turn sprouted, filled the territory with vegetation.

With the material obtained from the vegetation, Obatala created the first shelter on earth, even with the sound advice of Orunmila. The next step was the creation with the clay of human figures.

Only Olodumare, the creator of life, could "animate" them. In fact, after having descended to earth, with his breath, he gave soul to these clay figures, motionless and lifeless, all this under the attentive and envious gaze of Obatala. As a punishment, Olodumare made him sink into a deep sleep and continued the work of the divine creator started.

From the story of the creation of the earth according to the Yoruba tradition, it can be said that Olodumare "sees all and knows all," ***he is a learned and wise deity.***

Olodumare is also called "*Arinurode Olumoranokan,*" which means: "*one who sees the outside and the inside, and understands the intentions of the heart.*"

Many times its figure comes approached to Olokun, like an eventual rival, but erroneously, because being the supreme creator, he is placed on a higher level than any other Orishas. His virtues and powers are an example to all. He has no rivals and is ***unique***.

Yoruba culture celebrates Olodumare as ***immortal*** because he has always existed and will continue to exist forever. He is the giver and preserver of life and therefore cannot die.

He also grants immortality to the souls of mortals, and he also has the power to guard the souls after death and preserve them until he decides to reincarnate them in another body.

Olodumare is the king who "works to perfection," has immense power, and is ***omnipotent.***

Anyone can address and dedicate prayers to the divine, and he will be able to give answers to the invocations and help through Orunmila.

Other Names of Olodumare

Olodumare is known in the Yoruba world by other names as well due to how he manifests himself to humanity. Names are used in praise and prayers.

Some religions that arrived in Africa later, such as Christianity and Islam, have "adopted" many of the names attributed to Olodumare as names to indicate God.

Olorun

This is the version of Olodumare, sovereign of the heavens and the skies. He dominates the abode of the Orishas. The Orishas need his intervention to descend into the realm of men. The prayers are addressed to the sky because it is where the Orishas live and act as an intermediary between the faithful and the sky, mortals can not reach the sky, which is reserved for the Orishas, only after many sacrifices and a change of form, you can think of accessing heaven.

Olu'ase

This name means Olodumare as the source of all power and authority.

He is the source of all Ase, and without his Ase, no one else can function.

As the creator of all authority, Olodumare is also prayed to and hailed when a new king is proclaimed in the various Yoruba communities.

The king is prayed to manifest both his mortal authority and his divine authority, which is represented by the creator of all, Olodumare.

Olulana

Olodumare is invoked by this name when confusion reigns. In

fact, Olulana means "the one who shows you the way."

Olulana is a fundamental figure for the faithful who are confused about which path to take for their salvation of the soul or the resolution of life's problems.

Eledaa

It is the creative aspect of Olodumare, the creator and giver of life. The Yoruba people pray to him and praise him to protect them from curses and bad luck.

Elemi

He is the guardian of life, and it is believed that this figure lives between the physical and spiritual realms and has the function of being the intermediary between mortals and Orisha and mortals.

ORISHAS

Orishas are generally spiritual or supernatural entities that are worshipped by humans – particularly the Yoruba people. While the native Yoruba call them Orisa, which is pronounced as Orisha, variations exist in certain places where the Yoruba culture has permeated. For instance, the Yoruba community in Cuba identifies Orisha as orichá, while the Brazilian Yoruba culture of Latin America recognizes Orisha as orixá. The existence of the Yoruba culture (albeit varied) in other nations and foreign lands points at the thriving resilience of the culture – it is one of the few cultures that has been posited to stand the test of time and shake off extinction.

The belief that people don't utterly die but become guardian spirits that can influence the destiny of the living, and the fact that there exist other spiritual entities aside from those referred into the Yoruba culture leads to a question - are all spiritual entities Orisha? Evidently, the answer would be. Not all spiritual entities are Orisha. But even that answer would need a bit of explanation.

First and foremost, the defining attribute of an Orisha is they are worshipped. It is not just a matter of being a spiritual entity, but more of being a spiritual entity duly worshipped and reverenced by the living. Put into consideration a salient Grecian belief – the gods demand our worship, so they can be empowered and willing to intervene in our lives. The secret of gods and goddesses is in the fact that although they have a considerable measure of power and influence over the physical realm, they need the recognition and reverence of mortals to enable them to exercise such influence. Their relevance is mostly tied to the reverence they derive from mortals.

Having noted the core definition of an Orisha being mortals worship them, it stands to reason that although there is a spiritual realm with uncountable spiritual entities roaming, only those recognized and respected by and in the Yoruba culture are known as Orisha.

Although Orishas are spiritual entities that are regarded in the Yoruba culture, certain categories are worthy of mention. Orishas are not just guardian spirits of ancestors worshipped in a particular family. Neither are they just divine spirits superior to certain other spirits being worshipped.

First Class Orisha

The first level or category of Orisha belongs to divinities. Starting first and foremost with the "Lord over all" – Olodumare, who is also known as Olorun – Lord over the heavens (skies) Olodumare sees all, knows all, created all, and is all-powerful. Every other Orisha serves as a subordinate through which mortals can access Olodumare. He can be likened to Zeus, who is the head of the Greek Pantheon.

Still within the first category are other heavenly deities subject to Olodumare. These include Obatala, Orunmila, Osanyin, Obaluaye, Esu (pronounced Esu), among others, and existed before the creation of the Earth and its inhabitants. They're the ones known as Ara orun – the people of the heavens (skies), and they have greater amounts of power and influence than other Orishas below them.

Note: Irunmole is often mistaken as Orisha because they're spiritual entities that are recognized and sometimes worshiped in the Yoruba culture. They differ from the Orisha in one respect – they're mostly messengers of Olodumare who are appointed specific tasks on the Earth. They were neither born on Earth nor do they die on Earth. They simply exist on Earth for the duration of their assignment and ultimately return to Olodumare once their task is completed.

Divinities subject to Olodumare, such as Obaluaye and others, are often recognized as irunmole consequent on their spiritual origin, earthly appearance, operations, and eventual departures. They served as the link between mortals and Olodumare while on Earth and were the first visitors of Earth once Obatala had finished creating the Earth and the first Yoruba men and women. Ultimately, their return to heaven created a communication vacuum between the mortals and Olodumare, which was ultimately solved via special worship and invocation attributed to them.

What is utilized in invoking this irunmole (such as shrines and graven images) is referred to as Orisha because these items carry the presence of specific irunmole. While Orisha strictly refers to divine entities and spirits that are worshipped in the Yoruba culture, the Irunmole is a special category of Orisha still within the first class, subject to Olodumare and invoked through unique means.

Deified Mortals

These were mortal men and women, kings, warriors, hunters, healers ancestors who held great influence over the Yoruba culture by virtue of their sacrifice, personality, and powers. People like Sango were renowned kings who were deified by their followers and ultimately became Orishas. For a mortal to be deified, they must have shown great skill or power, which greatly affected the Yoruba community. As a case study, Sango was one of the fiercest kings in Yoruba's history, marking lots of territories and winning a lot of battles for the Yoruba people. Peculiar to his name was his affiliation to thunder, lightning, and fire. Sango Olukoso is the Orisha or Yoruba god of thunder and lightning. He breathes fire and summons lightning without rainfall or storms, thus striking fear and reverence in both enemies and subjects' hearts. His wives, Oya, Osun, and Oba, were renowned women who became Orishas commonly attributed to water and other feminine traits.

Note: Certain mortals became deified not based on their own strength or prowess but based on the spirit in them. These were known to be marked by divinity, i.e., they were reincarnations of certain Orishas. Thus, they possessed the unique traits of a number of Orishas. They were often not referred to by their names but by the names of the Orisha that marked them.

Natural Elements and Other Spiritual Entities

The Yoruba pantheon is made up of major and minor Orishas. The greater Orishas are strongly known and idolized in the Yoruba culture, while the lesser Orishas are not very well known. Divine beings with great power but possessing no human forms and manifesting through natural elements and phenomena are often classified as messengers of the first class of Orishas. They are mostly worshiped by a relatively small group of followers (these groups were mostly made up of direct descendants - each family had their own Orisha whom they worshiped apart from the major Orishas of the Yoruba pantheon). These lesser Orishas are what make the Yoruba pantheon vast and innumerable. Some are partially known by few, some exist and are known, but their followers have disappeared, and some exist but remain largely unknown. Be that as it may, these other spiritual entities are mostly regarded in the Yoruba culture as inactive Orisha, who is also known as house deities.

As stated earlier, every natural force or element has a spirit attached to it, and the Yoruba people love to pray to whatever spirit is behind any natural element or force to gain some form of favor or to avoid falling into it. Harm or incur anger for sinning against that spirit (knowingly or unknowingly). Natural forces such as water, fire, air, earth, metal, light, darkness, plants or herbs, and wild animals are duly respected in Yoruba culture because they enjoy the coverage of specific Orisha.

Cases where a mortal has witnessed an unnatural manifestation in a natural element often hinted that an Orisha had touched such a natural element. Due homage must be paid to that Orisha or spirit behind the unnatural manifestation. Numerous Yoruba tales abound concerning mortal men and women who heard voices from the waters or forests or picked up certain incomprehensible sounds from the land and air. Whenever such sounds or voices were heard, the default modality of such a Yoruba person was to beg for mercy not to be shot to death by the presence of an Orisha in such natural elements.

Note: Although there are major Orishas such as Osun, Yemoja, Orisha Oko who rule the natural elements, there are lesser-known Orishas that manifest and are worshiped through natural elements.

Colors of the Orisha

Another classification of Orisha is based on the colors attached to them. The colors hint at the personality and powers associated with such an Orisha, and it often influences the rituals to be made when invoking them.

Universally, the color white is used to symbolize peace. The Yoruba culture also recognizes this and attributes the color to select Orisha. Where an Orisha is associated with the color white, such an Orisha is known for peace and wisdom. An Orisha using the white color can easily be called upon without fear of suffering wrath. Such Orisha includes but is not limited to Obatala, who is also known as Orisha Funfun, Osun, the goddess of beauty, who is affiliated with water, and Orunmila, who is associated with wisdom. Yemoja, who happens to be the mother goddess of water, is also associated with the white color but is mostly depicted in blue – a pointer to her affinity with water, natural resources, and motherhood.

Where an Orisha is depicted in red or black, such an Orisha is often characterized by terror. They are usually fierce and warrior or hunter-based, calling for rituals that most often involve the spilling of blood. Utmost care is required when invoking a red or black-themed Orisha. Error or carelessness in calling upon such an Orisha could result in being struck to death by the Orisha. This category of ferocity includes Sango, the god of thunder and lightning, Esu, who is often called the devil, and at other times the trickster – is the god of balance and justice. Ogun and Aganju, among others, are likewise listed under this category. Patron gods of hunters, warriors, and blacksmiths are also depicted with the colors red and/or black.

Depending on the color affiliation, each Orisha possesses its unique ritual, food, object of invocation, dress style, and at times even requires a unique hairstyle from its devotees. For example, Sango devotees are noted for plaiting their hair and fixing white cowries in between the braids – this is in honor and replication of their patron god Sango who did the same.

It should be noted that the white-themed Orisha are known to be calm and wise – which explains why they are referred to as Orisha tutu (cool). But that doesn't deny them the capacity to require certain blood spilling for special sacrifices – after all, the seal of blood is the most potent. In the same vein, the Orisha associated with red and/or black, which are known as fierce, tasking, and generally scary – Orisha gbigbona (hot-blooded), can on rare occasions call for unique sacrifices that may not be "hot."

HOW TO WORSHIP THE ORISHAS

Prayer is very important in the life of a believer, but most importantly, they must pray to all the Orishas. They have to make a prayer with their work. Making this prayer is an offering. It can be done without a model, or it can be made on a small piece of paper.

Orisha prayer:

-The following words are used to pray to the Orishas, for example:

"In Your name, I make a prayer" "I offer this to you, O Orisha." - The Orisha is saluted with respect. Some add a brief prayer of thanksgiving or praise in honor of the deity. There are many forms of thanksgiving prayers. Some religious texts can be used as a model for praying.

- The expression of praise and gratitude that is used in the Yoruba language can be summarized in the following:

- "I thank you for what you have done and your help," "Thank you O Orisha," "Thank you, O Orun," "The Orisa is well." -

There are some words to be used in prayer to each deity. In general, these words are not pronounced exactly as written.

-There are four main types of prayers that are common to the Yoruba-Lucumí religion:

• The prayer of thanksgiving is also referred to as praise.

• The prayer of petition. This is the prayer "to ask for something."

• The prayer of obligation or gratitude for what has been given. It can be both petition and thanksgiving at the same time, depending on whether it is asked for something or simply praise. The prayer of obligation is often referred to as the "prayer of the Trinity" because it contains elements of praise, petition, and thanksgiving.

• The prayer of blessing, invocation, or consecration (which is done before making an offering).

Simple Prayers

The simplest form of prayer is as follows: "thank you spirit for what you have done for me" "thank you spirit for your help." Some people use formulas from which they choose words that summarize their petition, but these prayers are more compact and efficient than those that use more words or phrases.

- Statement: "I offer this to You, O Orisha."

- Statement: "In Your name, I make a prayer."

- By saying the names of the Orishas and their titles in a chorus, for example: "I offer this to Ochún. In His name, I make a prayer."

Model of Prayer

A model of prayer is a tool for beings. It is used as a way to be sincere, to practice, and to make things easy. A model can be made from any of the following materials: wood, metal, etc. The material depends on the Orisha that will give you their protection and blessing. However, it can also be of any color – black – white – red – brown – green – violet – orange – blue – yellow — but always decorated with leaves and fruits; flower petals; beads (snake, coconut shells, etc.) and colors (blue and yellow).

Every Yoruba religion has its own model of prayer. The Yoruba prayer to Orisha is given. It goes like this: "I want to work for Orisha, so I will do my best. Thank you, Orisha." This is the most effective prayer. It must be ready to work for everyone for life, so it must be done every day without fail, morning and evening. The first thing that Yoruba does when he wakes up is to pray to all the Orishas before anything else.

The prayer with the aid of the model is very effective. It is like a book of charms, and it can be read throughout your life. For this reason, people save it, and they need to know how to make it; because if something happens or you come out of trouble, you will be able to use it at any time. The model can also be used as a gift for special occasions.

The following are examples of the model of prayer to Orisha with different colors.

Examples can be made in any material, but wood is very good. The following are some examples:

The colors used in the model of prayer to Orisha are different depending on the specific color of your religion or religion that you want to access when you pray. If it is white, use oval beads for Ajowain, round beads for Oshun, red beads for Yemaya, and so forth.

The model of prayer to Orisha has mystical powers that can be beneficial. By praying, you can have knowledge. You do not understand all the words in a prayer, but sometimes a word means a lot of things, so it is important to know what is being told with your model of prayer to Orisha.

This type of prayer helps you communicate with the spiritual world and helps it open doors for you so that you can solve problems as well as opportunities as they come up for your life. If you have a problem, take the model of prayer to Orisha and ask the Orishas to help you solve it.

The model of prayer can also be used as a personal amulet. In this case, not only will you use it as a way to pray, but it will also protect you from things that may go wrong in your life. It can also be used in the way that you need something to help you in your day-to-day life, things that are bad for you, or even health problems.

The model of prayer to Orisha is not only used to pray to Orisha, but it can also be used in order to attract good things. Depending on the color of the bead, it attracts specific energies. The different colors of the beads are white, red, yellow, and green.

A model of prayer to Orisha can also be used if your pregnancy is having difficulties or you are unhappy with the life of your child. If you pray with the model to Orishas, you will help your children.

Prayer is very important in all religions, but not all faiths have their models of prayer. There are people who use the same model they used before they became Yoruba followers or who just improvise independently.

Prayers are said almost every day, even if they are improvised. This is because these prayers have energy, and you do not know where it will come from, but those who make prayer models to Orisha can tell you how to make their model of prayer by saying the name of the Orisha and the color of the bead.

The Yoruba religion allows its followers to talk to the spirits, but they have to do it with respect and love. If you pray every day with your model of prayer to Orisha, you will see that life will change for the better.

In addition, by working from a spiritual point of view, the results are very efficient and effective over time.

The models of prayer can be made by anyone who is open to learning about them. However, they are not free, but they do not cost too much to make. It all depends on the material you use to make it. You can ask an Orisha for help or consult a Babalawo to teach you how to pray with your model of prayer to Orisha.

The materials are usually round metal beads, ceramic beads in the shape of cubes, rectangular shapes in glass, or ceramic. Any material can be used, but these are the most common ones.

The model of prayer to Orisha can be made by anyone, but it is more effective if it is done by experienced people. It is always better to do it with the help of an Orisha or a Babalawo.

There are different versions of the prayer to Orisha, depending on which region or region you want to learn about. This is because each region has its own culture, traditions, and religion. However, all have the same goal.

The models of prayer are available in different stores, which are stores that specialize in the sale of Orisha items. These stores are called botanicas or tiendas Yoruba. They can also be found in markets that sell traditional medicines since they have a large variety there.

The Yoruba religion has a model of prayer to Orisha that is made by the community, and it is used only by the community.

Ashe

"Ashe" has the meaning of "so be it" and is a symbol of power and authority. Faith towards an Orisha must also be shown through the word and not just through an action (sacrifice). Every believer must know how to do this. Using an Ashe, one can determine the fate and even ask the Orishas for help. Some of the more popular Ashe may sound like this: "I am asking you for your glory, your blessing, and my protection." There is no limit to the number of times they say, but that depends on each person.

The more they say, the better. All communication with Orisha must begin with this prayer. It is also used when dealing with a situation where you need help, guidance, or a solution to a problem. After the Ashe, there is no need to say more, but you will have to wait for your Orisha's response or blessing, so it will be shown by them.

It is also thought that Olodumare blessed the human figures created by Obatala with Ashe.

The act of invoking the Orishas is called "Iboru." Once invoked, they tell the disciples things about their lives and the situations they face. The method of invocation is very important because each Orisha has his own way of being invoked. You can choose the one you feel comfortable with.

The circle of the Ashe

The "circle of Ashe" is an act of Purification, which is done by recording the name of the Orisha in the circle. This means that you dedicate your life to the Orishas and to God.

The circle can be done with all kinds of materials (paper, coconut stems, etc.), but it must be very colorful; leaves, beads, fruits, flowers, shells, snakes, or other items that are used to decorate it with colors. The circle of Ashe is prayed with water, milk, or other materials that are appropriate for the Orishas. It must be done that the eye is turned towards God and then prayed aloud.

Acacia (Ikú)

"Ikú, I offer this to you; please come to me; take my life; make it healthy; make it beautiful; make me happy and take care of all my family.

"Ikú, please help me. I offer this to you.

"Yemò! Yemò!

Ebo Riru (Sacrifice)

"Ebo riru" (sacrifice) is one of the most important things in the Orisha religion, which is symbolic and carries many meanings. It contains food prepared by believers for their Orishas according to their daily needs; fruit; flowers, honey, water, etc., more or less depending on the true relationship between them. The Ebo riru is done as a sign of love and respect to their gods. In addition, it is also a way of asking the Orishas to give them what they have asked for. The Ebo can be done twice a day, at sunrise and sunset, which is the time when the Orishas awake and go to sleep. This is done at a public place or in a private place that belongs to him or her. It can also be done twice a month – Once every 20 days – once every 40 days – one year – 5 years – 10 years – etc. It depends on what the believer decides to do it. The Ebo is also done when there are special events in the life of the Orisha, for example, when they are married, have children, when they are ill, have good fortune, or have misfortune.

There are different kinds of sacrifices that can be made. For example, The Ebo is usually done with food or other things that can be given to an Orisha or a Babalawo. That gift can be given to the Orisha or the Babalawo one time, or it can be distributed over time. There are full Ebo which are done with food, drinks, and drinks made with food items.

There are also partial Ebo which are done with one item of gift to an Orisha. That gift can be given to them once or several times. You can distribute it in several locations or give it all in one place.

Orisha sippets are the bread that is made from "Yemò" and placed under the hearth to thank Orisha for their blessings:

•"Ibo" (food) is the most important and sacred part of the sacrifice. Food used for sacrifices must be prepared by an "Osú," which is a believer who has to show sacrifices.

• Ebo riru can include more than one Orisha. They can be old – young – males – females – dogs – cows – dogs, horses, and other animals. It is important that it will be done in a public place where people can see it, but no one should enter the room where the Ebo riru takes place. The reason for this is that once someone enters the room, they will be seen by everyone, and this may cause problems for them.

• The Ebo riru also has something significant for believers to know: nobody should interrupt their Orishas when they are doing it.

A sacrifice is sometimes a complex act. For this reason, a priest or a faithful expert could help you in case of doubts or help you prepare your sacrifice.

Cowrie's Shell Divination (Obi Divination-Diloggun Divination)

To use Ashe effectively, experience and practice in cowrie shell divination are important.

"Obi" is a shell that is very similar to the sea snail. It is used as a type of amulet. In Nigeria, cowries are also called "Dagbani," which means "man's eye." It is believed to be the messenger or helper of the Orisha. The belief that it works as an amulet comes from the fact that people have been using it for divination since ancient times. The cowrie shell has various meanings. It can be used for love, luck, business, and friendship, to talk to Orisha, to answer prayers, etc.

Cowries are also used for divination. They are worn on the back of the neck (on the temple), and they act as an amulet for some people who ask some questions about their life or problems that they face. This is not an act of purification or any type of worship. It is done with good intentions only.

It is said that the cowries are the messenger of Orishas because it is believed that when you have a question for an Orisha, the answer will be found in them. Clean cowries are used for good things, while dirty ones are used when there is bad news or when they have problems to deal with. The cowrie's shell can also be used in case there is a need to determine if someone has been speaking behind your back. To do this, the person who is interested in knowing if someone had spoken behind his or her back must put an egg under his or her pillow. The next day, he must go to a river with clean cowries and ask them the question. If the answer is negative, then there was no one who had spoken against him or her. If it was positive, then there was someone who said something against that person's interest.

The cowrie's shell has many meanings, but the most significant are luck, love, communication, business activity, and family. There are many types of cowries of different values, and they can serve different purposes. For example, the larger of the cowries of the same color (black or white) shows an increase of whatever power it symbolizes: family, money, business, etc. The shape of the shell can also determine what power it has. Usually, the most expensive and rare type of cowries is the white "tiger," while the black "the buffalo" is less valuable.

The cowrie shell has many positive meanings, but it can also be used in magic. The belief about the spells that are done with this shell comes from Africa. They believe that when you use cowries to cast spells, they must be worn on the neck of the person who is to receive them. This causes problems for people who try to cast spells in bad ways. Because of this, there are many superstitions related to cowrie's shells. For example, there are people who say that these shells will cause sickness if they are worn on the wrong person. If someone tries to buy them for magic use, the seller must see his or her intentions. The seller must also ask if he or she is doing it rightly. When cowries are sold for magic use, there is a separate person who controls their distribution to ensure that this does not happen.

There are still many superstitions related to cowries. They say that they must not be thrown against the wall or they will break into pieces, and people's life will be in danger. They also say that when a person gets them, and they lay them on the table (and they don't know what to do with them), this means that someone will die or be seriously injured. It is believed that cowries would not dare to leave the house if these events happen.

Cowries shells can also be done with the following purposes: to tell if someone is true; to show that people are enemies; to know who is using or abusing money; to determine if someone will be content in their marriage; etc.

Obi is a type of necklace that can be made from cowry shells, but it is not actually cowries. The sellers of the shells have to ensure that their origin is from Africa. This is because if they are from another origin, they will not be authentic cowries.

Obi comes in different colors and sizes. It can be done with glass or plastic beads, metal elements, or shiny semi-precious stones. The beads used for this necklace are coconut, wood, or glass. Obi can be done on a regular basis or as an accessory to the attire. Obi is believed to bring good luck to women. The main color of Obi is red because it is associated with fertility and procreation.

Obi comes in many patterns, but the most common ones are: "Idemo nu," which means "gift of Orisha," or "lele epo," which means "I carry the cowries." These come in white and black colors. The white Obi is usually used for good luck, while the black one is more for bad luck. "Idemo nu" can be done with cowries of different animal patterns.

The origin of the Obi necklace comes from Africa. In Nigeria, it is very popular among women. It can be worn by any woman, but it has more meaning for older women who are married or divorced. It is important to note that not all Obi necklaces are made from cowries shells.

The cowrie shell (Obi divination-dilogun divination) is one of the most important tools that Orishas used to answer questions for their believers. It's like reading omens; it can be done on a daily basis or on special occasions. They are used to serve the Orisha Oya (the patron of travelers). It is an agreement between the Orisha and their believers to serve them in this way. The results are always positive because it is a shield against negative forces in the world. Human beings have the ability to communicate with their gods through this method, but they cannot control what is given by them since she governs by themselves.

Her believers must respect her decisions. It works as follows:

- Having the cowrie shell in the palm of your hands, close your eyes, ask your Orisha to speak with you through it. Open your eyes and look at the cowrie shell that you have on your hands. Try to see what happens to it (which way it falls, if it is on the left or right, etc.).

- If your Orisha is Ochún, you can ask her for seven answers because that is the number of cowrie shells that come in her Obi. If you are talking with Yemaya (the patron of the sea), you can ask for five answers because there are only five cowries shells in the Obi. This same rule applies to all Orishas travelers). It is an agreement between the Orisha and their believers to serve them in this way. The results are always positive because it is a shield against negative forces in the world. Human beings have the ability to communicate with their gods through this method, but they cannot control what is given by them since she governs by themselves. Her believers must respect her decisions. It works as follows:

  – If your Orisha is Ochún, you can ask her for 7 answers because that is the number of cowrie shells that come in her Obi. If you are talking with Yemaya (the patron of the sea), you can ask for 5 answers because there are only 5 cowries shells in the Obi. This same rule applies to all Orishas.

WHITE ORISHAS I

Power comes in many forms, and the Orishas are divided into two groups based on their expression of power.

White-themed Orishas are those who have a calm and peaceful demeanor, while Red / Black colored Orishas are known for their brutal and bloodthirsty expression of power.

Colors do not identify an Orisha as evil or good, but the choice is based primarily on each Orisha's preferences which color he would like to be associated with.

A substantial difference could be sought between the various rituals and sacrifices of the faithful in honor of the Orishas, but here too, there are some peculiarities.

Blood sacrifices, performed during propitiatory rituals, are recurring to honor the red/black-themed Orishas.

For the white-themed Orishas, the typical sacrifices made are food (ebo riru) or similar.

However, it should be noted that it is not excluded that the rituals with blood sacrifices can be performed for a "white" Orishas and that the less bloody sacrifices cannot be performed for an Orishas associated with the red/black colors.

It depends very much on the nature of what is required of the Orisha.

This highlights how the choices of the devotees' actions are characterized by the situations, the reason for the sacrifices, and many other circumstances. The certain thing is that the greater the request/need, the greater the sacrifice required.

We can conclude that the colors do not identify an Orisha as good or even evil.

OBATALA

In some myths, Obatala is said to have fought battles with a trickster named Yemoja. Their fight lasted a long time until Obatala threw Yemoja's cap into the ocean. He then made a bridge from the ocean to land and called upon all gods to come and worship him. In this way, Obatala was able to dictate what people could worship, which shows his power as one of the major deities of Yoruba culture.

In the beginning, there was nothing but the ocean, and when Obatala came forth from the ocean, he created people from clay and gave them specific tasks. In this way, Obatala showed his ability to take on human characteristics and was able to create different kinds of people who could accomplish different tasks throughout time. Obatala also chose from among his creations which ones would be descended into royalty. The ones that belonged to royalty were more powerful than the rest of the people because of their royal bloodline.

Obatala is considered a father figure in most African cultures because he created people in his likeness out of clay. This is an example of symbolic magic that the Yoruba have employed throughout time.

Although many things can be attributed to Obatala's powers, it is generally accepted that Obatala represents wisdom and magic. It is believed that Obatala has the insight to understand the true nature of all things and that he is able to change anything with this knowledge.

He controls the fertility of cattle and produces children through people who worship him (in this case, they become mothers). It is in this respect that Obatala may seem like a very ambiguous deity in a way because he controls these things in a way that is not necessarily good.

In the Yoruba culture, Obatala is regarded as one of the most powerful deities because he is seen as an all-knowing god that has the power to take on any form at any point in time. This can be interpreted from him being able to appear in both male and female genders and from his being able to control people's emotions and opinions which means he must have strong empathy. He also seems like a god that has wisdom and is able to see what mistakes were made in the past and how they could be avoided in the future.

Obatala is also seen as a father figure because it is stated that he created people to be like himself and that he is the source of all fertility in people. This means that any child that was born was given this ability by Obatala to create children in the same way. Thus, if he were ever angry or offended by someone who worshipped him, this could lead to infertility and ultimately the end of mankind (i.e., destruction).

Obatala is often depicted as being bald. His hair is sometimes described as being straight, or sometimes it is described as made of different colors. The symbol of Obatala's power over people's fertility may be associated with this because Obatala can take on the characteristics of women, which symbolically represents his power over women's fertility.

Obatala is also linked with the moon because he is considered a deity that controls women's cycles and menstruation. In Yoruba culture, women are often thought of as a reflection of a man's success, and Obatala is considered to be able to represent male virility. As such, it is said that men maintain their strength by worshipping Obatala.

Some religious scholars view Obatala as the mediator between humans and Olodumare, the creator god of the Yoruba religion. This mediation would explain how he saw things from all perspectives and had insight into every situation. This role also means that Obatala was one of the most powerful deities in Yorubaland because he was able to influence what both gods and men thought and how they acted on those thoughts.

Obatala is mainly known for its affiliation with the white color.

Orisha Funfun, as she is also known, derives from her name, Oba (meaning king), t'ala (which refers to an undyed fabric - a white canvas on which other colors are cast to represent its different paths). He is considered the light of all consciousness and the embodiment of purity, both physical and spiritual. Obatala is the Orisha adored to find purity, peace, and harmony in life.

Off the coast of southwestern Nigeria, Obatala is seen as Jesus of Nazareth because he is seen as the savior and protector of humanity. Like other Orisha who have reincarnated in humans, according to the Yoruba belief, Obatala was once Oba (king) of Ife. His subjects revered him until he lost the throne to Oduduwa. His loss of the throne is still the subject of dramatic history today during the Itapa festival in Ile Ife.

If the male Orishas' paths are greater than the female paths, Obatala is known for the existence of double paths. His paths are similar in number between males and females. Although the female ones prevail more, the Obatala priestesses are more numerous than the male priests.

Obatala also has a minor influence in the depictions of Santeria, Voodoo, and Hoodoo. There are only small variations, and these are seen essentially in the names and oriki. For example, if in the

Yoruba culture, it is called Obatala or Orisha Funfun, in these other religions, it is known as Orixala, Oxala, Ochala, Oshala, or Orichala.

Purity of heart is essential when invoking Obatala. Obatala will never respond to people with bad intentions.

The food that Obatala prefers in rituals are coconuts, milk, white bread, white rice, and water, accompanied by prayers or praising him with his oriki. Like Olodumare and other Orishas, Obatala reveals himself in several forms known as paths or avatars. These paths have different purposes and, as such, can be requested on the basis of specific needs.

Path of Obatala

Obatala is depicted in several forms known as paths or avatars. These paths can be requested based on specific purposes and needs.

Obatala Orisa Aye

It is a female path of Obatala and represents the great mystical virtues of women.

Obatala Ondo

It is a feminine path of Obatala, who lives near the rocks by the sea.

Obatala Ayalua

It is a path of Obatala represented as a destroyer, warrior, and exterminator. Obatala Ayalua is a rival of his brother Ayalá.

Obatala Alabalashe

It is a path where Obatala converses with his children with prophetic dreams. It depicts the past, the present, and the future.

Obatala Olufon

Obatala in this path can not remain in darkness. He needs continuous light. His shrine must always have a source of perpetual light.

Obatala Oloyu Okuni

This path of Obatala is the source and possessor of the eyes of all humans.

Obatala Osha Orolu

This is the king of the Egwadó.

Obatala Okelu

This path is the king of Ekiti and Abeokuta; he lives in the highest place.

Obatala Ana Suare

This is a male path of Obatala who accompanies Oba Moro. His sons cannot oust anyone from their home or raise their hands in anger.

Obatala Oshalufon

It is of the king of Ifón. This male path of Obatala gave people the ability to speak

Obatala Oguiniyan

This male path of Obatala does not allow anyone to see his face.

Obatala Obalabi

This path of Obatala is the Creator of Oyó and is supposed to be deaf.

Obatala Elefuro

It is a female path of Obatala. She is the queen of the earth and is also known as Imolé.

Obatala Oba Ayiká

This path of Obatala protects the houses. We rely on this path when we want special protection of homes and property.

Obatala Oba Malu

This path of Obatala is a help in the most difficult moments. It is a support for people to overcome obstacles in their lives.

Obatala Efun Yobi

This path of Obatala is the protector of his children and also those of his enemies. She brings serenity into the home and relieves leg pain.

Obatala Alarmorere

This Obatala path is depicted with a silver saw and hammer.

Obatala Orisha Yeye

This is another Obatala female path believed to be one of the oldest of the Obatala female paths.

Obatala Ogbon

This Obatala path walks with her brother Oggán. It is responsible for the journey of the spirits of Obatala's children when they pass through Orun

Obatala Aikalambo Male

This Obatala path is near Ibadánè and is the king of Iká. Originated in the Odu Ofun Sa.

Obatala Oshereilbo

This male Obatala path continuously walks with Sango.

Obatala Airanike

This path is called Ajósupato in Arará and is a warrior walking alongside Oshalufón.

Obatala Oyu Alueko

A male path of Obatala who selfishly does not want any Orisha to have children besides himself.

Obatala Orisha Iwin

This Obatala path originates from Owó and defends the palace of Obatala.

Obatala Oye Lade

This Obatala path represents a hunter and the king of Ekiti. In the Arara, his name is Bajelo, he always walks with Oshosi.

Obatala Ekundire

It is a men's path from the land of Iyesá and guides Oduduwa.

Obatala Orisha Obrala

A young and valiant male path from Obatala.

Obatala Bibi Nike

A male path of Obatala constantly riding a horse.

Obatala Edegu

This Obatala path is the king of the Efushé lands.

Obatala Abgany

This path is a master of Iyebú. He lives in the water, is blind, and is a defender of life.

Obatalá Ayenolú

It is a male path, also known as Yelú and Laguelu, in the city of Ibadán.

Obatala Agguidai

A male path of Obatala oversees messages with Olofi. It has four stones and instruments that are sealed and cannot be touched by the sun, air, or dew.

Obatala Orisha Aye

It is the path of Obatala that gave balance and order to the world and also brought the secret of Ase to Orunmila.

Oriki Obatala

There are different ways to approach Obatala. Simple prayers can be made to his name, and ritual meals can be placed before his shrine. But one of the easiest to do, which is most recommended for new worshippers and enthusiasts of the Yoruba religion, is to sing praises to the Orishas. These praises serve as a unique form of prayer and are known as 'Oriki.' Each Orisha has at least one oriki dedicated to him/her. Some are available to the general public and sung during festivals dedicated to the Orishas, but other oriki are sacred and only sung by experienced devotees and within closed circles.

Below is an oriki dedicated to Orisha Obatala:

Iba Obatala
Iba Oba igbo
Iba Oba n'le Ifon
O fi koko ala rumo
Orisa ni ma sin
Orisa ni ma sin
Obatala o su n'nu ala
Obatala o ji n'nu ala
Obatala o tinu ala dide
Adiniboiti ri, adupe
Ase, ase, asese o

This translates to:

Praise to the chief of the white cloth
Praise to the chief of the sacred grove
Praise to the chief of the heavens
I salute the owner of the white cloth
It is the owner of white light that I serve
It is the owner of white light that I serve
Chief of the white cloth sleeps in white
Chief of the white cloth wakes up in white
Chief of the white cloth gets up in white
He who creates at will, I thank you.
So, let it be, so let it be, so let it be done.

Another fascinating piece of Oriki for Obatala:

Obatala, the strong king of Ejigbo

Seating at the trial, a tranquil judge.

The king whose every day becomes a feast,

The Owner of the brilliant white cloth.

Owner of the chain to the court of heaven.

Obatala stands behind the people who tell the truth,

The protector of the handicapped,

Oshagiyan, the warrior with the handsome beard.

He wakes up to create two hundred civilized customs.

It is he who holds the staff – Opasoro, the great king of Ifon. Oshanla (mighty god), grant me a white cloth of my own

You who makes things white,

Tall as a granary tall as a hill.

Ajaguna, deliver me.

You're the king that leans on a white iron staff.

ORUNMILA

Orunmila is one of the most important Orisha of the Yoruba tradition and was sent to earth by Olodumare to initiate and complete creation, reclaim the earth and make it habitable to begin life. He is also known as Orunla or Agboniregun, and in the santeria, he is linked to St. Francis of Assisi.He is the son of Obatala and Yemu and is a relative of Shango and Eleggua.

Knowledge, divine wisdom, and justice are typical of the figure of Orunmila. His wisdom about him is so immense that he understands everything there is to know about human nature and has the most effective methods of purification. He founded divination and has his own form of divination known as Ifa (the divine wisdom of Olodumare).

Ifa divination is accessible only to a select few who are dedicated to learning and who can divination using Ifa as an oracle. Devotees to Ifa divination are the Babalawo (priests of Ifa) and Iyanifa (priestesses of Ifa). According to the Yoruba tradition of creation, it was the Orisha who advised Obatala on how to proceed, how to create the dry soil and mold man from clay. After the creation of man, Orunmila joined the other Orishas to visit the earth. He remained among the Yoruba people as a priest to teach the ways of righteousness, the characteristics and virtues of Olodumare, and the ways to invoke Olodumare. His divination powers are always precise and help determine a person's fate.

Orunmila has a special place among the Orishas, and this is mainly due to the fact that Olodumare has attributed to him the virtue Ori (intuitive knowledge). This special and unique power gives him the ability to influence and intercede in the life and destiny of each chosen person, and he can do so much more than other Orishas.

Realizing that his stay on Earth was not eternal, Orunmila knew that there was a need to fill the void that his absence would create. He foresaw this and gave selected people a greater portion of his wisdom, teachings, and divination skills. These people were to serve as priests in his stead once he left the surface of the Earth. They had to uphold his teachings and guide all who sought Olodumare's wisdom regarding their lives and difficulties.

The elect was given the title Awo Ifa which translated can loosely mean "the priest of Ifa." Suppose priests were mostly adult males who had undergone sacred training. Gender restrictions have been shattered over time as some women have shown potential in Ifa divination.

In fact, even females were allowed to participate in sacred training prior to their full initiation. The females had the unique title of Iyanifa, which can loosely be translated as the divination of Ifa's mother, instead of being called Awo.

Male and female are fundamental for existence and balance; in fact, duality is a principle in Ifa divination.

The basic principle is that the male cannot exist without the female essence, and the same is true for the female who cannot exist without the male essence. Precisely for this principle, just as the males had to be initiated into Ifa divination, the females also had to be initiated. Interest and being personally chosen by the oracle play a key role in being initiated.

Orunmila is a soothsayer who can predict anyone's fate and is characterized by great moral integrity and wisdom. As a result, devotees are expected to have a path in a life marked by honesty and loyalty, to live harmoniously and prevent problems.

Orunmila can rewrite fate, but only with the consent of the person concerned; otherwise, there will be no change in fate.

To celebrate this divinity, the rites of the devotees provide for a particular type of propitiatory dance and the offering of some types of food of animal origin, such as the hen.

Oriki Orunmila

Orunmila Eleri Ipin

Ibikeji Olodumare.

Akeju Oogun,

Obiriti, apijo Iku da,

Oluwa mi, atoibajaye

Oro abiku jigbo.

Oluwa mi, ajiki.

Ogege agbaiye gun.

Odudu ti n du ori emere,

A tun ori ti ko sunwon se,

Amo iku,

Olowa aiyere,

Agiri ile ilogbon.

Oluwa mi amoimotan,

A ko mo o tan ko se.

Aba mo o tan iba se ke.

Mojuba akogda,

Mojuba aseda

Akoda ti n ko gbogbo aiye ni Ifa

Aseda ti n ko gbogbo agba n'imoran

The translation is:

Orunmila, the witness of fate,

The second in command to Olodumare (Supreme God).

You are far more effective than medicine.

You are the one who averts the day of death.

My Lord, the almighty to save.

The mysterious spirit that fought death,

Unto you salutations are due first in the morning.

You are the equilibrium that adjusts the forces of the world

You are the one whose exertion it is to reconstruct the creatures of bad luck.

You are the repairer of ill luck.

He who knows you becomes immortal.

Lord of the King that cannot be deposed.

Perfect in the house of wisdom.

You are the lord who is infinite in knowledge.

By not knowing you in full, we – your servants are futile.

If only we could know you in full,

All would be well with us.

I praise the first created

I praise the creator

The first created who teaches the whole world the divination of Ifa

The creator who teaches the elders wisdom.

Odu Ifa

Orunmila already existed before the creation of the earth and was of great help to Olodumare in the role of a priest when he sojourned on earth. In fact, he is considered by the Yoruba culture to be the greatest priest who has ever been on earth and the creator of the divination system called Ifa.

Odu Ifa is a collection of 16 main books, and each book has 16 subdivisions of secrets that only the priests and priestesses of Ifa can access. Many think that the 256 Odu Ifa contains all the possible decisions and situations which can arise in everyone's life every day.

A sacred collection of Orunmila's prayers and stories handed down over the years by priests and priestesses, who gave advice and guidance to anyone seeking their help.

Regardless of the sacrifices that may be required to remedy whatever situation one may find oneself in, works of righteousness, also known as Iwa Pele, have often saved someone from total damnation.

Ifa divination prayers are divine and can only be reached by the priests and priestesses of Ifa. But here is a more generic prayer dedicated to Ifa. It is directed towards the human Ori (spiritual thinking), fundamental to the destiny of each individual.

Ori, mo'juba (I honor you and give you thanks),
It is you who is with me through all the events of life.
Ori're l'ori mi (I have a good Ori – head)
Ori ire (good Ori) that links me to Olorun
Ori ire that is Olorun's essence in me.
Ori ire that is open to receive the blessings that Olorun sends to me
Ori're l'ori mi (I have a good Ori – head),
Ori ire that is open to the wisdom of Ifa
Ori ire that is open to the guidance of Orunmila.
Ori ire that receives assistance from the Orishas – gods.
Ori ire that welcomes and embraces Egungun – the spirits of the dead.
Ori ire that welcomes assistance from Egungun.
Ori're l'ori mi (I have a good Ori – head)
Ori, I beseech you to keep my doors open
Ori, I ask that you always bring me blessings

Ori, I beseech you to always support me in tough times,
Ori, I beseech you to always rejoice in good times with me.
Ori, I embrace you, and I ask that you always embrace me.

Ashe, Ashe, Ashe o (a variant of Amen – so let it be).

WHITE ORISHAS II: THE GODS OF WATER

According to the Yoruba culture, there is a powerful balance on earth between masculine and feminine energy. Feminine energy was of crucial importance for the creation of the world; otherwise, it would have been an incomplete world.

Women have a quiet nature and a destructive one, and this can be crucial on many occasions, depending on the influence women want to address.

Men naturally have more destructive energy, and the influence of quieter female energy can have a beneficial effect on men.

For these characteristics, but also for their beauty and inventiveness, most of the Orishas women are associated with the white color and the element of water, and Osun is a prime example.

The Orisha Oya is an opposite example and highlights that Orisha women are not only associated with beauty and stillness but can also reveal ferocious and devastating power. In fact, she is associated with the color red, which symbolizes her violence and brutality. She is actively involved in the military campaigns of her husband Orisha Sango, and her thunderstorms have often helped Sango send lightning bolts to enemies during battles.

OLOKUN

If Olodumare is the creator of all Orisha, Olokun is the creator of every female Orisha, and in particular, those that have to do with the element of water.

Olokun is a hero who later became Orisha (a demigod) and is known as the "God of water" and protector of deep waters because he presides over the seas, streams, lakes, rivers, and rain in the Americas. He is considered a god of vision and revelation. He is a revealer of secrets and a bearer of prophecies. He can also do it on behalf of others.

He has the distinction of being androgynous but operates predominantly as a female Orisha. Olokun holds material riches, psychic abilities, dreams, meditation, mental health. He embodies many human characteristics such as meditation, patience, future visions. He is invoked to bring about fertility, prosperity, and health.

He is the god of fish and fishermen. He watches over those who go to sea and protects them from danger and evil. Sacrifices are made in honor of Olokun by those who want their prayers answered, mainly asking for success in work and protection in daily life.

In the past, the Yoruba people believed that Olokun was one of their most powerful Orisha. They believed that since all the water came from Olokun, he had power over life and death and could impart wisdom and prophecy. His cult is still very strong today. Priests conduct Olokun rituals for all kinds of wishes, including wishes for good health, luck, love, power, and success.

Olokun is worshiped in Nigeria and Benin along with Mami Wata, as the two deities possess very similar character and nature.

Here are some statements about Olokun:

-Olokun is the ruler of the "bottom of the ocean," which means that he also rules the water sources that are under the earth.

-Because Olokun resides on the ocean floor, this god is not often honored or worshiped by people on land.

-The ocean is very important for Olokun's existence because it provides him with his food source, which are animals, fish, and crustaceans.

-Olokun is invoked by devotees when they need to find items that have been lost at sea.

-Olokun is also seen as a spirit of the deep and can be found in any swamp, river, or lake.

-Olokun is highly respected by the Yoruba because he carries the power of the ocean with him.

-Olokun is also seen as the protector of fishermen.

-Olokun is also mentioned in the prayers to Yemaya.

-He also represents wisdom, protection, and stability.

-Olokun is the Orisha of the sea, and therefore, people who live by the sea should be very respectful of him.

-He Helps fishermen have substantial fishing trips.

-He protects waterways so that people can travel through them safely.

-If a person is devoted to this Orisha, it is said that he can easily understand the mysteries of life and death.

Oriki Olokun

Olokun aje ti aye oba omi
Omi nla to kari aye
Osele gbe senibu omi ti koni momo
Gbogbo eni ti waje
E je ka kori si ile Olokun
Sanle aje
Iya eni to l'aje
Iya eni to l'aje
Ogbugbu ni so oni so boji
Alagbalu gbu omi
Alagbalu gbu omi
Eni ajiki
Eni ajike
Ai ri di Olokun
Ao mo bere re
Aje pe gbogbo omi
E fi ori fun Olokun gbogbo odo
E fo ori fun Olokun oba omi

The translation is:

The owner of the waters and prosperity – the
Queen of the realm of waters
The great waters that cover the Earth
A wonderful ocean that has no end
Whoever seeks wealth, let them go to the
house of Olokun who has abundant wealth
Mother of uncountable wealth
Mother of uncountable wealth
Waters without end
Waters without end
The one we greet when we wake
The one whom we cherish
No one knows the source of Olokun
No one knows her beginning
Prosperity calls unto all the waters
Let the waters bow to Olokun

Crown Olokun as the Queen of the waters.

YEMOJA

Yemoja for the world Yoruba is the Mother Goddess of the world. She is considered "Lady and Queen of the Waters" and the mother of all the Orisha.

Yemonja's name comes from the words Yey Omo Eja, literally "Mother whose children are fish."

The sea is home to lost and innumerable riches and, according to Yoruba tradition, Yemoja possesses the riches of deep waters. It is also said that every time she turns in her sleep, she gives rise to a new spring, which then turns into a river wherever she is paths.

She is the goddess of the Ogun River, the largest river in the Yorubaland territory of Nigeria, and is the counterpart of Olokun, an Orisha, androgynous, considered protector of African slaves transferred to the Americas and the master of the sea.

Yemoja (or Iemanjá) Represents motherhood, purity, fertility, and femininity. Motherhood is both physical and spiritual; therefore, it includes love, care, protection, and guidance. She is a mother figure and is sometimes compared to the Virgin Mary of the Catholic Church and the Afro-Cuban "Our Lady of Regla." Yemoja, as already mentioned, is everyone's mother, but she has a soft spot for her daughters (women) and offers help to cure them for infertility.

If sterile, women could make sacrifices to Yemoja, and, in return, Yemoja offered one of her eggs for fertility. She also cares about the aspect of childbirth, nurturing, love and healing. She is considered a calm and quiet Orisha and is associated with the colors blue and white. She is responsible for the waves of rivers and seas, and whenever a storm occurs, her devotees know that she is upset, so they resort to some sacrifice to appease her anger.

Fishermen and sailors pray to her when they travel or when they are fishing. With her blessing, a fisherman is protected from the adversity of the waters, and she can hope for a great harvest of fish. Survivors of the shipwreck tell of being rescued by force and some of having seen sirens or heard sounds.

Yemoja is depicted as a beautiful Nubian woman walking on the surface of the water under a full moon or as a mermaid.

She generally holds in her hand a fan in gold and mother of pearl, embellished with beads and shells, and wears a beautiful necklace of blue crystals like the sea. The shells are sacred, and the places of veneration of her are the shore of the sea or of the great rivers that go towards the sea.

Among her features are the moon and the sun, the anchor, the life jackets, the lifeboats, and objects worked in silver, steel, tin, and lead that recall the sea. Her symbol is a six-pointed star, an open shell, and the moon.

The flowers attributed to Yemaja are violet and aquatic flowers, the fragrances of verbena, sandalwood, and dog-rose. Her animals are the creatures of the sea, the peacocks with their blue and green iridescence, and the goose. Her day is Saturday, and her number is seven, as the seas are seven.

Her stones are lapis lazuli, aquamarine, pearls, corals, and all the crystals of the color of the sea. In Salvador, Yemoja is celebrated together with the "Our Lady of Navigation" of the Catholic tradition.

Offerings of her as flowers, porcelain plates, jewelry, hairbrushes, etc., are deposited in her sanctuary in Rio Vermelho.

Yemonja was a spiritual entity charged by Olodumare to assist Orisha Obatala in training humans in the creation of the Earth. Yemonja descended to Earth with the other 16 Orishas of Orun on a rope and traveled the world, engaging with them in preparing the world for humanity.

Tapa (Iganna) in the Oke area of Ogun is the place of origin of Yemonja, and her worship began in Saki. Abeokuta, the capital of the state of Ogun (Nigeria), is the main site of her shrine.

Yemoja is often regarded as the wife of various male Orishas, such as Erinle, Okere, Obatala, Oko, and Erinle. Some also say that she is the mother of Ogun, Sango, Oya, Osun, Oba, Babaluaiye, and Osoosi, while many others say that she never gave birth but raised many children, most notably Dada, Sango, and Ibéji (means twins).

Yemonja is said to have taught other Orishas an alternative method of accessing the Odus, namely by "throwing" cowrie shells. She is very revered, and in her honor, there are several Yemoja festivals: February 2nd, September 7th, December 8th, or December 31st.

Paths of Yemoja

Yemoja Yembo (Yemu)

This path is the origin of the Yemoja crown and the mother of all Orisha. She is considered Oduduwa in female form.

Yemoja Ibu

This Yemoja path is married to Orisha Aganyu. Their encounters take place on the river bank.

Yemoja Ibu Oleyo

This path of Yemoja was born in Odun Ogunda - Iroso. She is always dressed in blue and loves fish and chickens.

Yemoja Ibu Olowo

This path of Yemoja was originated in the Odu Odi-Iroso. Yemoja Ibu Olowo is the possessor of all the riches hidden in the depths of the waters.

Yemoja Ibu Okoto

This Yemoja path originated in the Odu Merunla - Iroso. She is thought to live in shells.

Yemoja Ibu Asesu

This Yemoja path is the Orisha patroness of geese, swans, and ducks. She is Olokun's messenger and requires tolerance and consistency when she is called.

Yemoja Akere

This Yemoja path lives deep in the ocean and originated from the Odu Odi-Ojuani.

Yemoja Oro

This path of Yemoja acts mysteriously and works with egungun (masked spirit).

Yemoja Achaba

Born from the Odu Osa Mesan, this path of Yemoja is frequently represented as an anchor, but they often say that it is she who finds refuge in the anchors.

Yemoja Okute or Okunte

This path of Yemoja was born from Odu Ogunda Meji. She is a warrior, guardian of the Amazons.

Yemoja Mayelewo

This path of Yemoja is Olodumare's favorite daughter. She was born in Odu Irosun Ofun and lives in the depths of the ocean. She has stability as the main virtue.

Yemoja Ibuagana

On this path, Yemoja is the wife of Orisa Oko and was born in the Odu Iroso-Metala. Although she is very beautiful, she has seven protrusions on her abdomen, and one leg is smaller than the other.

Yemoja Atarawa

This is Yemoja's path, owner of the treasures found on land and in the ocean.

Yemoja Ibubunle

This path of Yemoja originated from Odu Eye'nle Meli. It is symbolized by a hook, a sword, or shells. Her home is the reef rocks.

Yemoja Ibu Akinomi

This path of Yemoja dwells in the waves of the water and was born of Odu Eye'nle Odi.

Yemoja Ibuconla

This path of Yemoja originates from Odu Odi-ejila. She is recognized as an inspirer for poets, and she creates ships.

Yemoja Ibuina

This path of Yemoja was born of Odu Osa-ogunda and is a warrior. She prefers goat and carp meat.

Yemoja Ogunayibo

This Yemoja path originates from the Odu Marunla-Ogunda. She is the Orisha patroness of older women and is famous for her large breasts. She is a warrior who works alongside Orisha Ogun.

Yemoja Ogunosomi

This Yemoja path works with Ogun and Sango. She was born from the Odu Iroso-obara. She is a warrior who climbs the mountain peaks and lives on the surface of the waters.

Yemoja Ibunodo

This path of Yemoja has a silver chain as its symbol, and her abode is rivers.

Yemoja Yemase

This Yemoja path has a mighty crown on which seven ritual cowries, machetes, and axes are hung. There is also a boat and an arrow by Orisha Oshosi.

Yemoja Ibualaro

This path of Yemoja can be represented as the Orisha of life and death.

Oriki Yemoja

Agbe ni igbe're ki Yemoja ibikeji odo
Aluko ni igbe're ki'losa, ibikeji odo
Ogbo odidere I igbe're k'oniwo
Omo at'orun gbe 'gba aje ka'ri w'aiye
Olugbe rere ko, Olugbe rere ko, Olugbe rere ko,
Gbe rere ko ni olugberere Ase!

Translation:

It is the bird that takes good fortune to the
Spirit of the Mother of the Fish – the assistant
to the goddess of the Sea (Olokun)
It is the bird Aluko that takes good fortune
to the Spirit of the Lagoon – the Assistant to
the goddess of the Sea (Olokun)
It is the parrot who takes good fortune to the Chief of Iwo
Children are the ones who bring good fortune from Heaven down to the
Earth
The Great One who gives good things,
The Great One who gives good things,

OSUN

In Yoruba culture, there are major Orisha that comes from the soil of the earth and represent different aspects of life.

The General Notes of Osun is a representation of beauty and fertility. In Yoruba folklore, Osun was said to have been both a goddess and a spirit in charge of women's fertility rates.

Osun can be seen as being responsible for periods in women's menstrual cycles, pregnancies, childbirth, and breastfeeding.

Many people in Nigeria use her powerful herbs to treat infertility-related issues; in addition, she is used by mothers for post-partum care when they breastfeed their babies.

General Notes of Osun:

"She is a powerful and sacred spirit. Her power is today manifested in her capacity to cure infertility and soothe motherly instincts. She reduces menstrual pains and helps to strengthen the intestinal tract."

"If one or more children are born as a result of a union with Osun, then that would be

considered as a gift from God, as the children were destined by God."

In Nigeria, General Notes of Osun is meant for those women who have been successful in having children after trying unsuccessfully for years. In other words, General Notes of Osun is not used for those who have miscarried or aborted their pregnancy. General Notes of Osun is also useful for women who have gone through tubal ligation and failed to conceive or those who did and were unable to get pregnant again.

Paths of *Osun*

Osun Ibu Kole

This Osun path works as a housekeeper and eats whatever sacrifices his vulture brings.

Osun Ololoridi

This path of Osun is a revolutionary and a fighter. With struggles, he seeks to create change.

Osun Ibu Akuaro

This Osun path has a secret name that only his children know, and he loves to eat with his sister Yemoja.

Osun Ibu Ana

This Osun path has the domain of the drums.

Osun Anani

This path of Osun is invoked to defend his case before the real help. It is a controversial path.

Osun Ibu Yumu

This Osun path is famous for its beauty. She is not courted because she is deaf, although it is not clear whether she is real or figurative deafness.

Osun Ibu Odonki

This Osun path abides at the mouth of the stream. She is the mistress of the streams.

Osun Ibu Ogale

This path of Osun is an ancient fighter who doesn't like to be disturbed.

Osun Ibu Akuanda

This Osun path was born in Odu Ikafun and is the one who freed Sango from Oya's kidnapping.

Osun Ibu Adesa

This path of Osun is the one who keeps the royalty. In fact, the meaning of her name is: "she who has the crown well secured." She is accompanied by a faithful peacock.

Osun Ibu Alade

This Osun path works closely with Eshu.

Osun Akuase Odo

In this path, Osun is said to have worked with spirits (especially those of the dead) as a stillborn.

Osun Ibu Bumi

This path of Osun has a personal Eshu that he works with.

Osun Ibu Eleke Oni

This Osun path is characterized by great beauty and excellent character.

Osun Ibu Itumu

This path of Osun is a warrior who rides an ostrich in battles. She is an Orisha protector of the Amazons.

Osun Ita Timibu

Osun's path is community leadership and only shows itself at night.

Osun Ibu Aremu Kondiamo

This Osun path lives on an Ifa divination table and originates from the mountain peaks.

Osun Ibu Seeds

This Osun path dwells in the areas around rivers.

Osun Ibu Fonda

This path of Osun is a warrior who died in the war.

Osun Ibu Odoko

Osun works on this path with Orisha Oko, and she is known as a peasant woman.

Osun Ibu Awuayemi

This path of Osun speaks through Odu Oyekun Meli: she walks with five bronze rods and a horse and is blind

Osun Ibu Idere Lekun

This Osun path inhabits caves and is delighted every time the waves crash against the ocean cliffs. To cover her flabby face, she wears a mask. It is the only path where Osun shows himself ugly.

Osun Ibu Inare

On this path, Osun thrives on wealth and is the daughter of Ibu Ana.

Osun Ibu Agandara

This Osun path originated in Odun Ikadi and is found with a padlock sitting on a chair.

Osun Oroyobi

On this path, Osun owns precious sands donated by Olokun. Her favorite ritual meal is salmon.

Oriki Osun

Oriki Osun Iba Osun sekese,
Latojuku awede we mo
Iba Osun Olodi,
Latojuku awede we mo.
Iba Osun ibu kole,
Latojuku awede we mo.
Yeye kari,

Yeye 'jo,
Yeye opo,
O san rere o.
Mbe mbe ma.
Yeye, mbe mbe l'oro.
Ase.

The translation is:

Praise to the Spirit of Mystery,
The Spirit who cleanses me inside out.
Praise to the Spirit of the River,
The Spirit who cleanses me inside out.
Praise to the Spirit of Seduction,
The Spirit who cleanses me inside out.
Mother of the mirror,
Mother of dance,
Mother of abundance,
We sing your praises.
Remain (exist), exist always Mother,
Exist always in our tradition.
So, let it be.

DARK ORISHAS I: THE TRICKSTER AND THE WARRIOR

D ark-colored (red or black) Orishas are often associated with devastation and cruelty.

They are known purely for their terror, and it is a basic reason why they are celebrated and worshiped by devotees.
It is true that they have a gory and intimidating temperament, but this statement is not entirely correct.

Dark Orishas, such as Aganju, Esu, Sango, Ogun, Oya, and others, are known for their brutal and heinous deeds, but that doesn't mean they are necessarily evil. Often the evil sent is directed towards the wrong people, or some wars are not caused or initiated by the dark Orisha. These examples want to highlight how many times the actions that are taken are a consequence of incorrect behavior on the part of the antagonists. Ultimately there is also a good end in actions that can be seen as senseless and wicked.

ESU

Esu has many names all over the world, from West Africa to Brazil (Eshu, Exú, Elegua, or Elegba), and is defined as the intermediary between the gods (Orisha) and humans, and a messenger between the Orisha themselves. He is a clever, irreverent god and always ready to make jokes and tease; in short, he is the trickster of the Yoruba tradition.

Esu is often seen as a complex character who can be both useful and harmful to humans. In fact, he is often referred to as a cheater due to his spiteful nature of him. He often tests men, deceives them, sometimes jokes or tempts them, with the main aim of helping them to mature. He is a god of causes and effects.

Esu is characterized by balance, law, and order, and for this, one pays homage to him in an attempt to attract his virtues into one's life. Considering his typically unpredictable personality, he can range from a benevolent spirit to a more chaotic and dangerous entity. He has an ambivalent character. On the one hand, he is spiteful, irascible, and violent. On the other hand, he often appears benevolent, cheerful, and protective.

Along with many other African deities, Eshu also crossed the ocean on ships loaded with slaves to stay close to his people in such a difficult time. We find him, in fact, in the Cuban Santeria and in the Brazilian Candomblé, where he is known as Elegba.

Many times Esu is depicted with a staff, representing power and order. His being changeable and capable of adapting to any situation makes him join the chameleon, the animal that holds the role of messenger of the supreme god Olorun. He is said to be adored for reasons such as protection, business success, political power, good health, and good luck.

Given his role as protector of responses and as a messenger, it is a good rule, whenever an important decision has to be made, to invoke Esu to orient himself in the right direction.

The virtue of his balance helps to clearly see the perspectives contained on the two sides, to evaluate the possible consequences, and make a correct decision.

Associated with medicine because it protects people with aneurysms, fibromyalgia, or epilepsy, who are often referred to as the children of Esu. It is also said that people with these conditions can heal themselves using herbs or amulets through the guidance of fortune tellers (Babalawo).

In the Western world, some religious scholars translate "Eshu" as "the devil," as an evil figure and even underworld, but all of this is extremely inaccurate. Esu, can be invoked through the Oriki in honor of him and offering a sacrifice of goats, black chickens, or coconuts. In many villages, there are shrines dedicated to him.

In conclusion, it can be said that the Orisha can be a divine help in the moment of making important decisions, and it is wise to ask for advice, but the final decision must be made by man.

Other features of Esu:

- Esu was blessed by Olodumare with the divine keys of each sacred door, so he is recognized as the first among other Orishas.

- Esu serves other Orishas, but he is the leader of the Ajogun.

- Esu is a mischievous Orisha, so he doesn't like monotonous people.

- Esu is known as Exu in Candomble.

- Esu is known by the name of Eleggua in Santeria.

- He is also known by other names in the Yoruba religions, such as Elewa and Elegbara.

- Esu is the first to receive a sacrifice before any other Orisha. Esu must be prayed before bringing a sacrifice to a particular Orisha.

Paths of *Esu*

Esu Laroye

This path is one of the youngest in Esu. He is a very good friend and messenger of Osun. He loves making jokes and is very mischievous.

Esu Lagu'na

This path of Esu is the patron Orisha of Egungun. He is famous for his strength of him.

Esu Bi

This Esu path is always seen at a crossroads. It causes discord and misfortune on people who make mistakes. His lessons are taught in painful and sometimes deadly deeds. He afflicts punishments if the lessons are not received. With him, it takes wisdom and foresight because Esu can be a great friend or a dangerous enemy.

Esu Anaki

This path of Esu is regarded as a female. He is seen as a guardian of law and rigor in the paths of Esu. She teaches how to make each path communicate with other Orishas and with humans.

Esu Aina / Bara Aina

This path is a messenger and works in symbiosis with Orisha Sango. He is tasked with paving the way for Sango when he goes into battle.

Esu Arerebioko

This path is the path that works with Ogun. Esu Arerebioko follows Ogun when he goes into the forest to hunt or during his adventures.

Esu Aye

This path of Esu has exposed the shores of the sea. He knows everything we want, so he is aware of the pleasures common to humanity and the secret places of riches.

Esu Elegbara

This path is very positive and blessed for its followers. It conveys luck.

Esu Alaketu

This Esu path is located in an area outside the city of Ketu (Africa). He is a wise man who bestows luck in the city.

Esu Afra

This Esu path originates from Arara, the land of Dahomey. Esu Afra is a great friend of Asojano.

Esu Ana

This path of Esu opens the way for communication between the Orishas and the sacred drums.

Esu Ashikuelu

This Esu path lives at the entrance to the market. He is a skilled broker and expert in resolving money disputes.

Esu Bara Layiki

This path of Esu is carefree, and he loves to dance and party.

Esu Dako

This path of Esu is based in the forest. He is a skilled connoisseur of hunting and herbs.

Esu Alboni

This Esu path resides high in the mountains.

Esu Ayeru

This path of Esu is the messenger of Ifa.

Esu Aroyeyi

This Esu path defends the entrance to Olofi Castle.

Esu Ode / Ode Mata

This Esu path marches alongside Ochosi in the hunt.

Esu Owo

This Esu path safeguards all the riches of the world.

Esu Beleke

This path of Esu loves to play, dance, and give fate to those who deserve it.

Esu Eluufe

This Esu path is old and wise. He is annoyed by those who have no respect for him. He grants wisdom, but only to those who are deserving.

Oriki Esu

Esu,
Esu odara,
Esu la'olu ogirioko
Okunrin ori ita
A jo langa lau
Arin lanja lalu
Ode ibi ija de mole
Ija ni otaru ba d'ele ife
To fi de omo won
Oro Esu, to akoni
Ao fi ida re lale
Esu ma se mi o,
Esu ma se mi o,
Esu ma se mi o.
Omo elomiran ni ko lo se.
Pa ado asubi da
Na ado asure si wa
Ase o!

This translates to:

Divine Messenger,
Divine Messenger of Transformation,
Divine Messenger speak with power.
Man of the crossroads, dance to the drum,
Tickle the toe of the drum.
Move beyond strife,
Strife is contrary to the Spirits of the Invisible Realm.
Unite the unsteady feet of weaning children
The Word of the Divine Messenger is always respected
We shall use your sword to touch the Earth.
Divine Messenger, do not confuse or hurt me,
Divine Messenger, do not confuse or hurt me
Divine Messenger, do not confuse or hurt me.
Confuse or hurt the child of another (instead).
Turn my suffering around
Give me the blessings of the calabash.
So, let it be.

OGUN

Ogun is the Orisha of iron and war. He is the guardian of all metals, especially weapons, which he uses to give strength to his followers. He is the protector of blacksmiths, hunters, metalworkers, artisans, and of the warriors who invoke him for victory.

A call to Ogun, whatever the situation, means victory is assured. He is a warrior god, skilled hunter, and above all, unparalleled blacksmith. According to the Yoruba tradition, Ogun is the Orisha creator of the paths and the first Orisha to have come to Earth.

It is said that the Orisha were unable to descend to earth due to too thick vegetation, but Ogun cleared the path for them, cutting away the tall grasses with his indestructible sword. It was always he who taught men metalworking.

He is often depicted in the pose of a warrior, holding a machete or a saber; in fact, he is considered the Orisha of the opening of the paths and the preserver of the peace obtained with the conquest. He, therefore, has the ability to open a path for anyone who has lost their way. His "warrior knife" is a short, heavy, sharp knife with a long handle and a harmlessly curved brass blade. He wears it on his left side tied to his belt. He also has a knife called a "cheating knife," which is a small, sharp blade that he carries in his right pocket. It is used to tease and irritate people when they annoy him or do things he doesn't like, such as trying to intimidate him, hold a grudge against him, or threaten him in any way.

Although he is the Orisha of war, he is not considered an evil deity but can be inflexible and ruthless, proud and warlike, but also protective with his proteges. The day dedicated to him is Ojo Isegun, the day linked to the battle, like our Tuesday. His sacred animal is the dog, from which he never separates, and on his sword, the oaths were sworn.

The Ogun cult involves the use of various types of iron objects during feasts and celebrations.

On the Ogun altar, in fact, we find tools such as weapons (swords, bayonets, spears), knives, pistols, ammunition belts, helmets, saw blades, hatchets, hard rags/leather gloves for protection during metalworking. Locksmith equipment, wrenches.

Although for Ogun, the dog is a sacred animal, the sacrifices made to it are not complete without the beheading of a dog held apart from the head and hind legs. Being Orisha's patron for hunters, he also requires sacrifices of bushmeat. Other forms of sacrifice are represented by kola nuts, palm wine, palm oil, roosters, salt (because it contains iron), snails, yams, alligator pepper, and water.

Non-devotees cannot pay homage to Ogun, but they can seek his blessing by turning to a priest or more experienced devotees.

Paths of Ogun

Ogún Onile

He is called Ogun Onile due to his nature as an explorer. His title means that he was the first to go to an uncultivated place, to settle and work the land—great Discoverer of animals, water bodies, and new territories.

Ogún Alagbo or Alagbede

It is a path that represents the patron Orisha of all blacksmiths. He has a rude and shrewish disposition and is always concentrated on work. He does not waste time and energy in conversations and is a hard worker.

Ogún Meji / Ogún Bi

This path of Ogun has two faces. The first has the appearance of a good and industrious parent who loves respite and serenity. The second face is aggressive, impetuous, and bloodthirsty.

Ogún Arere

This Ogun trail is a butcher.

Ogún Shibiriki

He is the figure who created all things in metal and is referred to as the killer. He is bold, proud, and very brave. He is jealous of Sango and is fighting for the love of Yemoja. He was born to fight.

Ogún-Kobukobu

This Ogun path is depicted holding a whip and is known as the foreman.

Ogún Aguanile

This Ogun Path is a conqueror and master of the mountains and new lands.

Ogún Adaiba

This Ogun Path is a conqueror who shows love through his machete.

Ogún Jobi

This path of Ogun is a violent warrior who also reacts with destruction. His characteristic is to hide among the brambles to ambush enemies or his prey.

Ogún Adeola

A proud and valiant warrior who became king. His main goal is to preserve and defend his people with wisdom and honor.

Ogún Já

This path is renowned for violence and is a fierce warrior. He eats dogs and is a great provocateur and aggressive. He prefers a bloodbath rather than a bath in water.

Ogún Oloka

This Ogùn path is also known as Olorukó. Owner of the land he works and of all that is cultivated and harvested. He is famous for his good harvests.

Ogún Aroyo (toye)

He is violent and impulsive. He is the best guard in the palace, as he always has quick reflexes and is quick when there is danger. He is irritable and deeply irrational.

Ogún Onira

This name was given to him because, on this path, he was king of the city of Ira. It symbolizes rain, mud, and the muddy waters of the river.

Ogún Onire

This Ogun path is known as an army general and a man of war. It was the king of the city, Ire.

Ogún Oké

This Ogun path is referred to as the protector and owner of the mountains. It is also called Afanamule and Ogún Ogumbí.

Ogún Aladú

This Ogun Path declared war on Yemoja

Ogún Valanya or Ogún Valenyé

This Ogun Path is known as the one that tills the land.

Ogún Niko

This Ogun path exercises the figure of the killer.

Ogún Olode

This Ogun Path is the leader of the hunters.

Ogún Soroka

This path is known as "the highest speaking" path.

Oriki Ogun

Ogun Lakaaye o!
Ogun alara ni n gb'aja
Ogun onire a gb'agbo
Ogun Ikole a gb'agbin
Ogun gbengbena oje igi ni'imu
Ogun ila a gb'esun isu
Ogun akirin a gb'awo agbo
Ogun elemono, eran ahun ni je
Ogun o, makinde ti n dogun leyin odi
Bi o ba gba Tapa a gb'Aboki
A gba Ukuuku a gba Kemberi.

This translates to:

Ogun Lakaaye o!
Ogun manifests in seven paths
Ogun of the town of Ilara is the one who accepts a dog for atonement
Ogun of the town of Ire will accept a ram for atonement
Ogun of the town of Ikole will accept a snail for atonement
Ogun of the town of Gbenagena drinks tree sap for atonement
Ogun of the town of Ila accepts yam seedlings for atonement
Ogun of the town of Akirin accepts the fleece of rams for atonement
Ogun of the town of Elemono eats tortoise for atonement
Ogun o, the brave that wages war with aliens/foreigners
He will destroy either Nupe or Hausa

He destroys alien/foreign people and will destroy Kanuri too.

DARK ORISHAS II: SANGO AND OYA

Death plays a significant role in the tragic love story between Sango, a mighty Alaafin of the Old Oyo Empire, and Oya, his concubine with powers to summon rain and transform into animals.

Their story is comparable to the Shakespearean story of Romeo and Juliet, where two minds in love see beyond the family feud and cling to their love. In the end, only death will seal their infinite love.

Sango is compared to many women in his life, but he is credited with two wives in great competition with each other, Osun, whom historians considered the legitimate wife, and Oba the second.

In Oya, however, Sango found something that both of them lacked, and in fact, it became her favorite. The bond between them is so strong that Oya is definitely more than a wife for Sango.

The bond between them strengthened thanks to the superpowers they possessed, and we can certainly say that together they were a powerful and invincible force. Together they are a devastating force, possessing powers that complement each other.

When it's time to defeat their enemies, Oya, who has the power to summon wind and storms, leads the attack, while Sango, who can give life to the fire of her thunder, can deliver the final blow to enemies and get a victory.

It was said that Oya was the one who advised Sango to get rid of her two prominent war generals, Gbonka and Timi Olofa Ina, as they refused an order from her.

Although Sango has brought great expansion and prosperity to the Yoruba kingdom, thanks to his great manhood and his brutal character, he has become its undoing.

There are various hypotheses about the end of Sango. The first (the most accredited) tells that his reign ended when, by mistake, he destroyed his palace with lightning, and this act was followed by a revolt of the people against him who asked him to resign from Alaafin.

For this reason, Sango fled the city along with its leaders and members of his royal cult called Baba Mogba.

Some say that Sango hanged himself in Koso on an Ayan tree, but this has been disproved and declared false by Sango devotees.

Anyway, Oya, Shango's favorite wife, the only wife who remained faithful to him to the end, took her own life for Sango's disappearance/death, just as Juliet did for Romeo, for the loss of him was powerful, and she had a pure feeling of love.

SANGO

Orisha Sango (pronounced Shango), known in Latin America as Chango (Xango), is the god of fire, the god of lightning, and thunder.

He is the representative of power and justice. For this reason, he is often represented with a double ax called Oxê (Oshe).

Sango was a historical figure, and more precisely, the third ruler of the Oyo Empire, one of the most flourishing in West Africa of the 15th century. Sango was a ruler devoted to war, and it is said that his reign came to an end when, by mistake, he destroyed his own palace with lightning to get the attention of the Orisha, who welcomed him among themselves.

Sango is the most terrible of the Orisha. It is said that thunder and lightning come directly from him, so when lightning strikes the ground or a rock and produces fragments, these are kept as talismans blessed by Sango. Sango is the spirit of war and physical strength. He represents strength, protection, masculinity, violent justice, and healing.

The fierce aspect he takes on when engaged in combat is often invoked by him devoted to him during times of conflict to become strong themselves. He is worshiped by warriors, athletes, hunters, and all who live according to the dominion of physical strength.

Orisha Sango is often invoked to grant virility to men who require "male fertility." Sango is a fiery Orisha of the Yoruba pantheon, so his predominant colors are red and black with blood-colored tricks.

Sango's energy must never be tested or challenged because he becomes extremely aggressive when provoked. He is a very active deity, and the more aggressive his energy becomes, the more powerful he becomes. He can be very violent in times of conflict, but he is always ready to administer pain and punishment to those who deserve it. The work he does when he is invoked can bring a lot of pain and suffering, but once completed, he heals many sick and wounded in him.

Statues representing Shango often show the ax the ox emerging directly from the top of his head, indicating that killing enemies and warfare are essential characteristics of him. Oxe is also used by the Sango priesthood. As they dance, the priests hold a wooden ax close to the chest for protection or swing it in a wide arc towards the chest.

The bata drum is Sango's signature drum, and he is said to have played bata drums to evoke storms and lightning. For this reason, during the evocations and prayers in honor of him, they are played by his devotees.

Sango has often been regarded as the symbol of blacks' struggle against white slavery.

During the 18th and 19th centuries, thousands of Yoruba people were enslaved and transported to the new world, and in many locations in the Caribbean and South America, African slaves and their descendants were able to restore the Sango cult. At the beginning of the 21st century, Shango was worshiped in the Santería tradition of Cuba, the Vodou religion of Haiti, and also the Candomblé cult in Brazil. Two new religious movements bear his name: the Afro-Brazilian cult Xangô, very present in the city of Recife, and Trinidad Shango (also known as Shango Baptists).

His followers braid their hair adorned with cowries. Sango followers offer cult foods such as gbegiri (bean soup), bitter cola, and amala during ceremonies. They are forbidden to eat cowpea, as this would provoke the wrath of Ogun, the god of iron and the patron saint of Sango Orisha.

Devotees worship Sango on the fifth day of the week, and he is known by the name of Ojo Jakuta.4 and 6 are the sacred numbers attributed to Sango. When a fixed object is struck by lightning, the devotees transform the area around the object into a sacred place for the Sango worship cult.

Paths of Sango

Sango Obadimeyi

This path indicates the relationship between Sangó and Aganju, the twin brother. Sangó and Aganju, being twins, must be followed in the same way.

Sango Obakoso

The title Aganju received after ascending the throne of Oyó, signifying the return of Sangó.

Sango Bum

In this path, Sango is represented as the son of Yemoja and Obatala.

Sango Dibeyi

This path represents the connection between Sango' and the children he had with Osún, known as Ibeyi.

Sango Alafi

This path of Sango is united with law, justice, government, and supremacy. Sangó Alafi is revered for his prestige and sense of justice.

Sango Arira

This path represents Sangó as the ruler of the rains. Bringer of peace and the one who ends drought.

Sango Olose

Sango Olose is the possessor of power and the double-edged ax, a solid and great warrior. He must not be contradicted because his words are law.

Sango Kamukan

He is the one who works with Egun and is in control of life and death.

Sango Obara

Sango Obara in this path is poor, and his clothes are of little value, but he never lies. His word is sacred. A house touched by Sangó

Obara's ray will be abandoned and cursed.

Sango Jakuta

Sangó Jakuta is a path of Sangó. It means "the one who throws stones."

Sango Ko So

This is a path of Sangó, meaning 'the one who did not hang himself.' This refers to the events that occurred after the death of Sangó, the fourth Alaafín of Oyó.

Sango Bara Lube

This path of Sangó was the master of divination before the advent of Orunmila.

Sango Olufina Kake

This path of Sangó is the owner of the Ceiba tree, the creator who sets fire to the streets.

Sango Obalube

This is a path of Sangó, where he met his wife, Oyá. It means "The king who attacks with a knife."

Sango Obaluekun

Sangó Obaluekun is Sangó's epithet, literally meaning "the king who hunts leopards.

Oriki Sango

Sango Olukoso!
Akata yeri
Arabambi Oko Oya
Alaafin ekun bu, a sa
Oloju Orogbo
Elereke obi
Eleyinju ogun'na
Olukoso lalu
Ina l'oju, ina l'enu
E'egun tin yona l'enu
Orisa ti n bologbo leru
San'giri, la'giri
Ola'giri Kankan figba edun bo.
A ri igba ota, sete
O fi alapa segunota
Ajisaye gbege oko Oya
Oloju Orogbo, Sango Olukosooooooo!

The translation for this is:

Sango the king of Koso,
The strong and mighty man.
Arabambi, husband of Oya.
The great and terrible ruler (of the palace) with a tiger.
The one with the eyes of bitter kola,
Whose cheeks are like kola nut.
Whose eyeballs are like coals of fire.
With fire in his eyes, and fire in his mouth.
The great masquerade that spits fire.
The god that is feared by all.
Sango the strong and mighty one.

With his might he reclaimed Edun.
He is unmoved by the sight of a thousand enemies.
He smites his enemies with his double-edged axe.
The one who awakens to impact the lives of all who call on him, the husband of Oya The one whose eyes are like bitter kola,
Sango - king of Koso.

There are various Oriki that speak about Sango in Yoruba folklore. In this, we shall include only a few of the most important ones.

• *"Sango baye ile saren de dere lotope lajibi, dinu dan. Nii sango dieno doewu loorun, daaduun sango"*

This translation is as follows: "Sango flies on a horse of iron, and he holds a thunderbolt in his hand. This is Sango, creator of human beings with wisdom and fortune."

This oriki expresses the fact that the awesomeness of this Orisha can be compared to that of powerful warriors such as those who fought for their kings in the Middle Ages.

• *"Ba sango bubu fian fujo olorun loloke sango, beni anu are raraa sango"*

This translation is as follows: "Sango's are songs are beautiful, songs heard by all people including the gods." This is speaking of the power of songs to affect change.

• *"Otu o a afa a Okun lo sango, orokun o Tolusfun o Oloru o Ejio"*

This translation is as follows: "Ogun and Olokun and Olorun and Elegba and Obatala".

This oriki is telling Sango to go and make an offering to Oloko, Osun and Elegba.

- **"Oluwo sango labi oko ni, fenu baa rano ne sango"**

This translation is as follows: "Oluwo Sango excites at the time of the war. He always terrifies. He is the god of war."

It is implied that this oriki was recorded when Oloko, Ogun, and Sango fought in the Middle Ages. It also could be speaking of the wars between these Orishas in modern times. *Sango is also called "divine creator" in this oriki.*

OYA

Oya, is a powerful and enigmatic goddess of the Yoruba world, is the Orisha who rules the greatest and most violent natural changes such as tornadoes, earthquakes, floods, cyclones, lightning, and even the wind.

She was Ogun's wife, but she later married Sango, the god of thunder. Oya is also the patroness of the tumultuous Niger River. She had nine children, the nine tributaries of the Niger River.

She possesses immense power, and sometimes in the depictions, she dances with weapons in hand, the machete, to chase away ghosts, as she is the only Goddess able to do so.

She can bring unexpected luck and therefore be a light that bursts into life. Her aspects of her are as numerous as her many colors: all of the rainbow, plus black and red. She is also called the lady of fire, a sudden, explosive fire, as she is in her character. For this reason, she is often represented with fire in her hand. Oya helps women overcome a fear of male figures and stand side by side with their husbands with honor and authority.

She is the Orisha bringer of many changes and often devastation; she is a guide for people to consider and rebuild. For these reasons, she is a goddess who cannot stand stagnation. To encourage change, she attracts a lot of attention. If that is not enough, she increases the intensity until she reaches her intent. It is the drive to make you leave the old and direct you to the glorious birth of the new. Oya is the air and the wind, and therefore the breath, in particular, the first and the last, hence her definition of a companion of the dead. This is why cemeteries are also called "Oya Gardens."

She is a warrior goddess. She is the patroness of the female ability to be authoritative and to rule. Oya is unpredictable, sudden as the wind, and she can go from being gentle and calm to angry and furious. If she cries, a pouring rain falls on the ground.

The cult of her, especially in Nigeria, is practiced by setting up an altar in the corner of the house and includes a clay vase covered and surrounded by amulets and various magical and symbolic objects.

The copper crowns, which symbolize the copper palace which she shares with Sango; a sword representing Oya's ability to deliver an effective speech; layers of red, brown, or orange glass beads, locust scales, and buffalo horns and represent symbols of the goddess. In devotion to the goddess, you can place a red and brown pearl necklace on your temple to sanctify her energy.

To fully please Oya, offer dishes full of foods she loves, such as akara, eggplant, or bean cakes. The invocations of Oya are made during stormy nights, sitting on dry ground, scattering purple and red flower petals, and with a lighted candle.

Reciting her oriki, you write on a piece of paper the changes you want, then ask the goddess to remove all the obstacles that are present in your life in order to arrive at the desire so that the spirits can get away.

Faith in Oya and her personal commitment will lead to the desired results.

Oya is known in Brazil by the name of Yansa, which is the bringer of fire. She is also one of the most important deities of Macumba).

In Cuba, she is called Olla, Aido-Wedo in Haiti, Brigette in New Orlean.

Paths of Oya

Oya Iyansan

This path is in reference to Oya, goddess of the storm. Known as the queen and source of the Niger River (in the Yoruba world called Odo-Oya)

Oya Bomi

This path of Oya is known as the one that can cause from modest winds up to tornado and hurricane-level winds.

Oya Afefere

In this path, Oya is known as the Goddess of

Her changes are not gradual but fast, brutal, and often destructive.

Oya Igbale

This path is known for protecting graves marked with crosses and cemetery gates.

Oya Ira

This Oya path is thought to have entered Ira's realm in search of Sango when he was informed of her death.

Oya Funke

This path of Oya takes in custody and protects the spirit of stillborn or unborn children while leading them into the afterlife.

Oya Iya Efon

This Oya path can be prayed when an illness is in its terminal state.

Oya Dira

This path of Oya is skilled with horses and is an experienced businesswoman.

Easy to find her in places where business is transacted.

Oya De

Oya De, after her death, became an Orisha goddess, but in life, she was an invincible warrior, and her skills were unparalleled.

Oya Nike

This path of Oya is known as the representative of women, as she has fought several times in their favor. For this reason, women often require Oya's strength to choose the right words to express themselves convincingly and authoritatively.

Oya Obinidodo

He is represented by a machete, the sword of truth. Oya will cut through all injustice, deception, and dishonesty in his path. He is in charge of guiding the dead to the cemetery and leaves their souls in the hands of Babalu Aye. He is present inside the cemetery, and the side gate of the cemetery belongs to him. Maintain contact with ancestors.

Oya Dumi

This path of Oya is considered the protector of children and spouses and is a tenacious and proud protector of women.

Oriki Oya

Oya yeba, Iya mesan, Iya Oyo.
Orun afefe iku lele bioke,
Ayaba gbogbo le'ya obinrin.
Ogo mi ano gbogbo gbun,
Orisa mi abaya
Oya ewa, Iya mesan.
Ase.

Translation:

Spirit of the wind, Mother of nine, Mother of Oyo,
The winds of heaven bring down the ancestors,
You're the queen of all women.
Always protect me with your strong medicine,
My guardian Spirit is the queen.
Spirit of the Wind and Mother of Nine.
So, let it be.

DARK ORISHAS III: THE HEALERS

In the previous chapters, we have analyzed the characteristics and virtues of the white Orisha, associated with calm and counsel, and the dark Orisha, known for judgment, often brutal and merciless.

We will now analyze a category of Orisha, which is in the middle of the two groups mentioned above, very important and decisive in the Yoruba world, the healers.

They possess the power to influence many aspects of life, but healers are Orishas who specialize in healing.

Among the main ones, we find Babaluwaye, who is the Orisha who heals all diseases. Osanyin the Orisha, who knows the properties of plants and specializes in herbal medicine, and Nana Buluku, who takes care of women. Babaluwaye is a dark Orisha, while Osanyin and Nana Buluku are white Orishas. Babaluwaye, being the Orisha of all diseases, is certainly the most charismatic and complex figure, which deserves a particular study.

In addition to having the power of healing, it is believed that he can rage on people who make mistakes, or for selfish reasons, even inflicting terrible diseases.

BABALUWAYE

Babaluwaye is the god of healing and is one of the most important and respected Orishas in Yoruba culture. He has many names, such as Babalú Ayé, Obaluwaiye, Obaluwaye. In the Yoruba world, Babaluwaye is depicted as a muscular man, with several sores covered in raffia curtains and with crutches, representing his control over leprosy, smallpox, and disease in general.

He is accompanied by two dogs, who lick his wounds, relieving the pain of his sores.

His story of him tells that he was initially respected and revered by everyone, but his unruly and stubborn behavior sealed his fate and his body. He was punished with illnesses and injuries, which he had to live with.

This lesson brought Babaluwaye to the right path, and he became the protector and healer of those who seek physical and even mental healing by invoking him. He is worshiped for preventing diseases. He is the healer of infectious diseases and is invoked to cure them. He is the Orisha who helps to preserve the health of all. Babaluwaye is the Orisha of life but also of death and is the patron of diseases. He can act in two ways: he can cure the sick, or he can inflict disease.

Even with modern medicines or medical technologies, if Babaluwaye inflicts a disease on a person, his anger and rage must be appeased in order to seek a speedy recovery. Worshiping Babaluwaye is a good start to achieving physical and mental well-being, but he must be helped, with a healthy lifestyle, perhaps by changing harmful habits and eating healthy foods.

The healer of all ills is the one who heals the body, mind, and spirit, and Babaluwaye has these characteristics. Babaluwaye is the healer par excellence. He is the Orisha to refer to when you need treatment. If you are depressed, he will propitiate your recovery. If you are sick, he will cure you. If your heart has been broken, she can mend it with her advice and her wisdom. If your life dream has gone wrong, Babaluwaye will help you chart a new path to follow.

His energy heals deep pain, soothes overwhelming emotions, and clears destructive thoughts. With him on your side, you can release any pattern that is holding you back from your true potential and achieve the success you seek. His energy also helps you release whatever is holding you back from achieving your goals, often held back by worry or fear. With his strength, it becomes easier to accept reality and at the same time seek what is yet to come.

Babaluwaye teaches that one should celebrate each day as it comes without wishing for any unlived day. He also teaches us that while change is often scary, it is necessary for your growth as a person. You should never allow yourself to be limited by anything other than yourself. He also teaches us to celebrate the things that make us unique.

Babaluwaye is an Orisha who can bring blessings when you have done good deeds and who can see your divine path in life. He helps you fulfill your destiny through her gentle reminders and pushes when you're off course. Babaluwayé is the healer of all ills, but he is an Orisha who helps stimulate your healing abilities, makes him stronger and more lasting. Humility is a key principle you must adhere to, as Babaluwaye doesn't like arrogance. Therefore, always be open and unafraid to say what you have in your mind and heart.

Babaluwaye is often prayed to in situations where sickness and death are present. He helps the souls of the deceased and brings peace and tranquility to their families. Babaluwaye also brings comfort to those suffering from all forms of pain, including heartbreak, depression, and physical ailments.

His power lies in his ability to heal mind, body, and spirit. He can restore health where he is deficient by making sure the right medicine is taken. His medicine is also good for helping ailments of the mind. When you call upon him, ask him to help you make peace with all things in life.

Invoking Babaluwaye

Babaluwaye is the orisha of healing and protector of health. He is called every time it is necessary to prevent or cure diseases, especially in the terminal state.

He has the power to heal, that is, to favor a death that can cause the least possible suffering; in fact, he is also invoked to help a sick person, with no more hope, to pass through a peaceful death. A Yoruba legend has it that he managed to heal Sango after no one believed in his healing anymore. This story was a demonstration of his immense and divine healing power. Babaluwaye is a great connoisseur of the healing power of plants, which is why he is associated with the Orisha of herbs, Osain.

Invoking Babaluwaye without being a priest is a serious mistake because you risk terrible diseases that can lead to death, so it is preferable that divination is done using the Diloggun or the Obi system of divination. Grain, tobacco, and wine are willing offerings, and invocations should be made, especially when the temperature is higher.

The offerings must be placed before the altar erected in his honor, with a statue representing him and decorated with candles and sacred stones for prayer, strictly for mercy.

It is approached Babaluwaye, in Santeria San Lazzaro, a leper of the Catholic tradition who was often represented with two dogs licking the wounds caused by his wounds. He is celebrated on December 17, just like Saint Lazarus. He is associated with the number 17, and his day of worship for him is Thursday. In tradition, he is depicted in bright colors such as red, brown, blue, purple, and black. Babaluwaye resides in an earthenware pot decorated with ciprea shells. Priests can invoke him by using the vase with 18 cypress shells.

All of Babaluwaye's worshippers are known as his children. They often suffered from skin diseases in their younger years. As we have already mentioned, Babaluwaye can be calm and healing, but also furious and nefarious, and this is also reflected in his "children," who can have healing power, both medical and spiritual, but also the power to inflict terrible diseases.

Here are some prayers that are recited in favor of Babaluwaye :

• *Babaluwaye, the god of all sicknesses and those who are sick.*
I call upon you, have mercy on us.
We are your children, have mercy on us,
Keep sicknesses far away from our homes, and protect us - your children - from all plague.
Thank you, father, for you have answered, and you will heal us.

Paths of Babaluwaye

Babaluwaye's paths are about 60, and Sopona is one of its most troubling paths because it is the path that names it as the Orisha of smallpox, a disease that in the past was fatal to a large number of people.

Here are the main paths of Babaluwaye:

Babaluwaye Asoyin Arara

It is the path of Babaluwaye, known as the father of rain, and has the power to kill with its particularly hot temperature. It is said to be the path that has killed many with smallpox.

Babaluwaye Alua

It is the path of Babaluwaye characterized by wisdom.

Babaluwaye Baba Arugbo

This is a path known as the ancient father and has the appearance of an old man.

Babaluwaye Afimaye

This path of Babaluwaye walks alongside Orisha Oyaè, who administers the dead. He is known as the mortician.

Babaluwaye N'yone Nanu

This is the female path of Babaluwaye Asojano. She lives in the ceiba trees and always wears a black dress.

Babaluwaye Molu

This is the path of Babaluwaye, representative of hunting. She often uses a bow and arrows covered in leopard skin.

Babaluwaye Aberu Shaban

This is a male path of Babaluwaye, who feeds on the intestines. He brings food to the children of Babaluwaye Asojano.

Babaluwaye Abokun

This is a male path of Babaluwaye and is depicted as a farmer and is always in the company of a lion, a crocodile, and the maja. He is known as the one who fertilizes the land.

Babaluwaye Adu Kake

This is a path of Babaluwaye in Cuba. He is depicted with the body of a man with the head of a dog and lives without clothes in the mountains.

Babaluwaye Adan Wan

He is a male path of Babaluwaye, very touchy and fierce. He kills anyone who offends him.

Babaluwaye Af'rosan

This is a male path of Babaluwaye, who uses the air for his activities.

Babaluwaye Afisinu Sanaje

This is a male path of Babaluwaye and lives in the market. He has the appearance of a mouse and speaks very little.

Babaluwaye Ajidenudo

He is a male path of Babaluwaye, who lives with Osanyin and supports witchcraft. He has the appearance of a dwarf.

Babaluwaye Amabo

This is a male path of Babaluwaye, who punishes sinners with elephantiasis and chickenpox.

Babaluwaye Apadado

This is a warrior path of Babaluwaye and lives in anthills.

Babaluwaye Bayanana

This is a female path of Babaluwaye and is the Orisha patroness of the virgin daughters of Babaluwaye Asojano.

Babaluwaye Ason'tuno

This is a male path of Babaluwaye and is popular for being a traveler despite being afflicted with many diseases.

Osanyin and the Differences with Babaluwaye

For the Yoruba, health is a combination of physical, mental, emotional, and spiritual well-being, and to achieve this harmony, they resort to divination to discover the cause and remedy of their disease. There are many healers, but the herbalist is the one who satisfies the needs of anyone who is sick by providing both diagnosis and medication.

Osanyin is a god of herbal medicine and a healing priest. Created by Olodumare to teach humans how to find remedies for their disease problems through the use of plants and herbs. He is a strong orisha and an excellent doctor, to whom plants are offered as a sign of respect and devotion. He knows all plants, their secrets, their use.

Osanyin is the Orisha who can show the way to identify diseases and teach how to cure them.

There are big differences between the Osanyin and the Babaluwaye, although, at first glance, they may have the same characteristics and be confusing. Obaluwaye is considered to be the true god of medicine, while Osanyin specializes in knowledge and care through plants. If you are looking for a path that offers knowledge and use of plants, Osanyin must be followed and adored.

Osanyin heals with indifference; Babaluwaye, on the other hand, often inflicts disease out of pure selfishness. In fact, he doesn't heal everyone, especially those on whom they inflict disease. Babaluwaye works through his raffia curtains which he uses as a broom to eliminate disease, Osanyin works through a power group.

A substantial difference between the two deities is that Osanyin uses plant medicine to relieve pain in the sick, while Babaluwaye helps the terminally ill to have a pain-free transition.

In conclusion, it can be said that these two Orishas are fundamental in medicine and that despite the differences of divine nature and powers, they can be an aid in case of illness or suffering for the world of the Yoruba faithful.

OTHER IMPORTANT ORISHAS

There are other important Orishas that are helpful to know. With so many Orishas, it can be overwhelming to understand what they all represent and their significance, but learning them gradually and in groups can be beneficial. These Orishas may not be as well-known as the other ones, but they still have fascinating stories and important roles in Yoruba religions.

OBA

Oba is a goddess whose symbol is water, and being as such, it makes sense that she is the goddess of rivers. Just like water, she is a dynamic and flowing orisha. Oba is a consort of Shango as well as the daughter of Yemaja. She is part of a trinity with Oya and Oshun, who are her sisters, and they all handle water as a source of life.

Some common traits of hers include flexibility, revival, energy, motion, and manifestation. A beautiful and rich goddess, she is prone to jealousy, but she is also hopeful. Her hopefulness can make her naive, and it can result in her falling for tricks when the trickster appeals to what she wants. Yet, she is not weak except to those who know her pressure points.

Her story is a sad one, and one of her greatest adversaries is her own sister, Oshun. While Oshun has a sexual relationship with Shango, as did Oya, Oba wants to be the sole love interest for Shango. However, because of her ability to cook, Shango likes Oshun best of all his women. Oshun, for her part, is resentful because Oba is the first legitimate wife of Shango, which means that Oba's children will inherit Shango's kingdom. That status isn't enough for Oba, though, so she seeks her sister's advice on how to please Shango. Because she is jealous of Oba, Oshun tells a tall tale about cutting off her ear and drying it to be sprinkled on Shango's meals; she promises that the ear will regrow. This story causes Oba to cut off her ear and put it in her husband's food. Shango then sees her ear floating in his meal, and he thinks she's trying to poison him. Filled with anger, Shango sends Oba away. Distraught over what happened, Oba fell to Earth, becoming the Oba river, which meets the Oshun river at a turbulent juncture.

Her story is often overshadowed by others, and that tendency reflects the tragedy of her story because despite her work to fulfill her passion and desires, she was unable to get what she wanted, and she was never number one in the eyes of the man she loved. Her desperations and gullibility are what get her into the most trouble; yet, she is not a complete fool. She is powerful and often times smart, but it is her yearning and want of love that makes her foolish.

Her exact associations vary across cultures. For example, in some parts of Africa, she protects sex workers, while in other places, like Brazil, she is considered to be a goddess of love. Frequently, she is related to domains like marriage and motherhood. Additionally, she is commonly associated with the colors pink and blue with some accents of red and white, and she is connected to the number eight and the days Friday and Sunday. She has a range of symbols associated with her, including wedding rings, flowers in her colors, headscarves, and double swords.

One holiday related to her is Kuomboka, which relates to the flood cycle that occurs each year in places like Zambia. Accordingly, she represents getting to higher ground and being safer from the potential dangers of water.

AJE

Aje does not have a clear gender, and to some is a god while to others is a goddess. However, for the purposes of this book, she will be referred to as a goddess. For those looking for abundance, Aje is an appealing goddess, and her connection to prosperity makes her one of the most worshipped goddesses of the hundreds of Yoruban gods and goddesses. Aje is the goddess of wealth, so she is worshipped for her bounty and ability to improve economic outcomes. She encourages trade and all types of currencies. She is also often associated with marketplaces. Aje represents much more than just financial wealth, and she's a bold and confident goddess. She rewards those who do good deeds, which shows her generosity and willingness to give prosperity to others. She especially rewards those who do goods to other people.

She is the daughter of Olokun. Her mother is Yemaya. As Olokun's only daughter, she is loved very deeply by her father, and Olokun appreciates those who will praise his daughter.

Aje is commonly found near water. She's usually found in white clothes, and cowries are part of her accessories, and this represents cowries being used as currency before there were modern currencies.

In one story, Orunmila tries to find Aje, and in his search, his patience prevailed because seeing that he wasn't trying to hurry to see her, she was more welcoming of his presence. When she sees desperation, she hides and does not grant prosperity. Thus, being patient is rewarded. Orunmila also gave Aje offerings such as bananas and other foods that she likes, which results in her rewarding him richly.

The Aje festival takes place on February 24 each year, and it is a special holiday to celebrate Aje. On this day, worshippers often bring white pigeons to celebrate. These pigeons represent purity as well as peace. These pigeons are used for prayer, but they are then released back into nature.

Aje is a powerful goddess who can offer wealth, but she expects those who worship her to act in goodwill and be patient. She shows that generosity and wealth can go hand in hand.

NANA BULUKU

Nana Buluku is the supreme goddess, and she is linked to the start of creation. She first showed up in Fon mythology, but she shows up in a range of religions, including the Yoruba religion. Her domain is primarily in West Africa. She is also known as a manifestation of Yemoja among some religious groups, but others say that Yemoa is a separate deity.

She is known for being courageous. She is also known for being a very rich woman who would help fellow women when they were having trouble with their husbands. This makes men afraid of her because she's willing to go out of her way to make sure that both women and children are treated appropriately. Her reputation results in her struggling to find male companionships. Men could not keep up with her strong character. She represents the image of a woman who will not be pushed around by a man and who can stand on her own. She resists the expectation that women be submissive to a man.

She is the daughter of Olokun. As Olokun's only daughter, she is loved very deeply by her father, and Olokun appreciates those who will praise his daughter. Another important part of her character is that she is the mother to twins Mawu and Olisa, who are the moon and sun, respectively.

One of her best-known associations is to Ogun, who is the God of Iron, who traumatized her. Ogun raped her, and at that point, she ran away to Dahomey. As a result of her rape, she dislikes iron and all objects made of it. Due to her own rape, groups often relate her to abortions and other issues with pregnancy. Sacrifices to her include drowning sacrificial animals and using bamboo tools to cut those animals.

OSHUMARE

Oshumare is a cosmic goddess related to the origins of the Earth and a supreme being. She is known as the connection between the Earth and the rest of the universe. She is associated with things such as creation, procreation, and rainbows. She's often associated with serpents. One interesting connection she has is to the umbilical cord, which is because it is known to connect things, including energy, nurturing, and the creation of life; furthermore, it relates to her being a protector of children.

She's often portrayed as a naked woman who sits with her legs crossed and wears a mask, which suggests that she is strong and mysterious. She has her arms held out, and a rainbow shines between her arms. She has an Earth in her lap that spins. The mask represents strength, and it shows her high sense of self and self-possession. She knows her own self, and she is willing to stand by what brings her joy and feels true to her nature. She never wavers in that respect.

Oshumare is a tranquil goddess. She is also proud, but not in an excessive way. She's all about balance. Thus, she is commonly associated with things such as Reiki healing, yoga, meditation, and chakras. She finds a deep connection with the universe, and through her connection, she can find internal peace, which she offers to those who worship her.

In some instances, Oshumare is not the usual god or goddess that you would expect, and she is said to spend some time as a male deity, and in various iterations, she is either portrayed as transgender or androgynous.

OSHOSI

Oshosi is also spelled as Oxosi, Ochosi, and Ochossi. His close friends are Ogun and Eleggua, and he usually isn't that far from them. Collectively, they are called "the warriors." As a hunter and a defended, Oshosi is linked to justice and is represented by his arrow and arc. He lives in the forest and is said to have the power to transfer himself to other locations so that he can take what he wants. As a wizard, he is often associated with witchcraft. He's commonly linked to the color blue, which matches the blue coral necklace that he wears that has some blue beads. He's also associated with yellow. Furthermore, he's linked to the number three, including multiples of three as well as the number seven.

He's a cunning adversary and is highly focused, but he also promotes balance between people and nature. He believes that we need to be aware of our surroundings to promote justice and help us grow better and evolve as people. He is highly knowledgeable about all the elements of nature. His skills allow him to not just be a provider for his family but many others as well. He instinctually knows how to hunt. His pet parrot contains his knowledge. This parrot is an important part of his lore.

In one version of one of his popular stories, Oshosi decides to hunt one day, but unfortunately, the animals around him a scare. He doesn't want to overwork his pet parrot, so he leaves the parrot behind with his grandmother. He goes into the forest alone to hunt, using the medicine that he has from his parrot. Eventually, he finds prey to bring back to the people he has to feed. He tries to find his parrot, but there are only parrots. He's devastated by the loss of his parrot, who he assumes to have been eaten by a hungry person. He sends out his arrow and tells it to hit whoever hurt his parrot. When he goes into his house, he sees that his grandmother has an arrow through her chest.

This story and its variations show his high standard for justice and his passion for making things right. It also shows much more than that, and it shows that in our search for justice, the results may not always be easy or turn out from what we expected. It also warns you to be careful about the people around you who may betray you. Oshosi can help you realize hard truths.

Oshosi shows that people are connected with nature. There are signs when we are in harmony and when we are disconnected from nature. He represents learning to adapt and have continued balance, even in challenging situations. In many ways, he directs people to be their best selves through this balance and wants to promote growth for them through his knowledge and guidance.

OKO

The Orisha Oko is another hunting deity and a protector of the land. He makes sure the land is fertile and is often linked to farmers for this reason. He is also linked to the balance between life and death because he has the power to sustain life, and without his blessings, life cannot be sustained. Oko is also a fair deity. He has a strong moral compass, and that drives him in his pursuits.

Due to his link to farming and all the hard work that goes into it, it is no wonder that Oko is a hardworking Orisha. He was one of the first Orishas to work on the Earth, and when he became exhausted by working the land and trying to tend to the Earth, he complained to Olofi, who promised that in time there would be other Orishas who would help him on Earth. Olofi also compared Oko's children to fingers on a hand because when they worked together, they could get more done. Through the death of humans, as their bodies are given back to the Earth, Oko gets rewarded for his efforts. It is him who returns people to the Earth when they have died, and in the process of human deaths, Oko is being fed by human bodies in the ground.

Oko and his family are known for their loyalty. His children are loyal to their father, and his relationship with his wife is strong. He is married to Yemaya Agana, and her marriage to her represents the ideal marriage, as it connects both the water and the land.

He is often symbolized by phallic objects in African religions, which symbolizes his association with fertility and sustaining life.

He's often associated with the color red. Some of his tools include plows and oxen, who can pull machinery for faster work on farms. He is linked to the number seven. Offerings to him can include root vegetables and smoked fish, and animal sacrifices include sacrifices of guinea hen, pigeons, and roosters.

ORI

Ori is an important Orisha in a range of religions, including Yoruba, Umbanda, Candomble, and Voodoo. What makes him stand out is that he can give people blessings instantaneously. He strongly represents a connection between our heads and the spiritual field. Thus, he has great influence over destiny, making him incredibly powerful. With his help, people can learn to heal themselves physically and spiritually. People tend to consult Ori when things are going wrong, and they want guidance to make things better and to promote a positive future. He helps people find balance in themselves, and he can help people promote prolonged well-being.

EGBE

Technically, an Egbe is not an orisha but is a related spiritual entity. Egbe, also sometimes called Egbe Orun, represents a group of spirits living in the Orun (heaven). To explain this more clearly, Egbe Orun means the spiritual mates of humans. This concept is often hard for people to understand because it is often abstract and mysterious. Each person has an Egbe Orun, no matter who they are or what they believe. Yoruban religions believe that all humans must have a spiritual force in the Egbe Orun and these spiritual forces are loyal to their human mates. They promote good things, and they help people reach their destinies.

HOODOO AND VOODOO

Hoodoo and Voodoo are words that people often use interchangeably, yet they are different practices, and each has unique beliefs despite some overlap. These practices are both popular in the witchcraft, healing, and magic communities, and there are negative and unfair connotations associated with these practices. One of the main differences is that while Hoodoo is a spiritual practice and a set of ancestral beliefs, it is not a religion, but Voodoo is a religion. This chapter will detail what each practice means and how they relate to Yoruban religions. The truth about these spiritual practices may surprise you and give you some insight into not only how they developed but what they mean to those who practice them.

HOODOO

Hoodoo is a spiritual practice that arose from the transatlantic slave trade, and it is folk magic for African American people, so its origins are in Africa. It is not a religion because it does not have an organizational system. These practices were used for enslaved people to continue their traditions and religious practices in secret, and it was a way to resist their captivity and hold onto their spiritual practices. These people's spirituality was one of the few things that they could keep of their own. These practices are highly related to secrecy, so many of the traditions are done at night and in private conditions. The power in Hoodoo stems from the suffering and perseverance of enslaved people who had to endure so much just to survive and carry on their family lines.

Hoodoo often links to Roman Catholic beliefs and uses the religion's saints, but practitioners will also incorporate the Lwas and Orishas;. However, Lwas and Orishas were not part of the original practices of Hoodoo because Hoodoo has evolved and expanded over time to capture other practices and new practitioners. The main spiritual connection is with ancestors in traditional Hoodoo practices, and it is an ancestral connection that continues to drive Hoodoo practitioners.

You should note that Hoodoo did not originally use Orishas, but it does have a lot of inspiration related to Yoruban culture. Many Yoruban ideas became foundational for Hoodoo practices, such as the deity Eshu-Elegba. During the slave trade, many of the names for deities and the lore related to them was lost; however, in Hoodoo, there is the belief of a spiritual entity at the crossroads, which is inspired by Eshu-Elegba. Another example of Yoruban influence is the use of iron in practices, such as using horseshoes, which relates to Ogun, the Orisha related to iron.

VOODOO

Unfortunately, Voodoo is often associated with evil and other nefarious concepts, but Voodoo is much more than most people realize. It is a religion with long roots, and its portrayal stems from colonial power struggles and fears of western forces. Many practices in the Voodoo religion became demonized by Westerners, who would exaggerate the traditions and make them seem evil, such as furthering rumors that Voodoo included human sacrifice. The media began to spread falsehoods, and as a result, Voodoo started to become something that it wasn't in Western culture.

Whereas Hoodoo arose in Africa, Voodoo was established in Haiti, and many practitioners may use the alternative spelling of "Vodou" to describe Haitian practices, while Voodoo is often related to Vodou practices that arose in New Orleans. As with Hoodoo, this practice was established as a way to promote spiritual freedom under oppression, and it was brought to the United States due to slavery.

Voodoo uses both Catholic practices as well as traditions from West African religions. It was a product of cultural clashes during and after the slave trade. This practice even was a factor in the first Haitian revolution that allowed Haiti to become independent from colonial France. Thus, Voodoo, because of its role in causing a colonial rebellion, those in power in the United

States and Europe started to associate Voodoo with negative forces. Thus, colonizers began to create a narrative suggesting that Voodoo was primitive and uncivilized.

In the United States, as black people started to get more power, the erroneous lies about Voodoo were used to further narratives that supported racism and white superiority. The history of Voodoo echoes the struggles that African Americans faced because of colonial forces.

However, Voodoo is an enriching religion for so many people, and the goal is to interact with deities in a way that promotes health and happiness. The Yoruban religion has influenced Voodoo despite the significant divergence and how these religions are practiced. Not all slaves were from areas that practiced Yoruban religions; yet, some of the deities, such as the warrior spirits like Ogun or Eshu, influenced Voodoo, and there's no doubt that the Yoruban people had a role in the formulation of religions like Voodoo.

CONNECT AND TALK
TO THE ORISHAS

The Yoruba people, mainly in western Africa, have a variety of cultural practices that reflect their belief system. One such practice is divination- which refers to the use of magical skills (a combination of mentalism and mediumship) for obtaining or establishing knowledge about something not visible or tangible, relying on chance operations, subjective analysis, or natural phenomena. Divination serves to explain or solve problems or serves as a form of communication between them and the gods.

In Yoruba culture, there exists a body of literature that comprises history, mythology, and folklore. This body of literature is called IFA and comprises 256 chapters as compared to the Bible, which comprises 66 chapters. The IFA has been in existence for several centuries with scribes/priests who are literate transcribing them in hard copy or in soft form (through recitation).

The IFA as a body of literature is a collection of Ifa aphorisms/proverbs, which were derived from the words of Orunmila, the god of divination and wisdom. These proverbs serve as words of advice and admonitions on various subjects ranging from wisdom to child-rearing to moral issues, thereby giving one a clear picture of how they should live their lives and what is expected of them.

It should be noted that divination did not begin with Orunmila but from the creator of all Olodumare. The Yoruba legend tells that Olodumare reunited his children and communicated that it was time to continue the work of creation he had begun.

From that moment, the Orishas would have had a method to communicate first with him, then communicate with each other, and finally with all humanity.

Their primary task will be to teach every living being his will and the means to be able to reach him spiritually. The change was also introduced by Olodumare to commission the growth of the planet he created and increase the number of devotees of the Yoruba people.

In the modern-day, these scribes are called Babalawo/Babalorisa, who is believed to be chosen by Orunmila himself in their lifetime. The Babalawo/Babalorisa has been described as being literate, open-minded, and of great intelligence.

Another major source of information about how an event or situation will pan out is through dreams. This is due to the fact that dreams are believed to have divine inspiration. There are two types of dreams among the Yoruba people, the first being "Ogbo Oru," otherwise known as "sickness dreams," and the second being "Eburu Oru," otherwise known as "good dream."

The first kind of dream, which is a sick dream, is a type of dream initiated by Orunmila himself through which he presents an opportunity for healing either spiritually or physically. The sick person who experiences these dreams will be offered advice on what he should or shouldn't do in order to be healed. Ifa practitioners among the Yoruba people usually interpret this type of dream for sick people and advise them accordingly.

The second kind of dream, "Eburu Oru," is a type of dream that is initiated by the person himself, which serves to foretell a happy or positive happening in his life. In this instance, it is not Orunmila who presents this opportunity for the person, but it is he who interprets the meaning of the dream. It will be him who advises or guides on what actions should be taken or what should be avoided based on an interpretation of this kind of dream.

The third major source for divination among Yoruba people is through interpreting oracles. The word 'Oracle' comes from the Greek word "Oraculum," which means a dispatch or a message in the form of a question and a prediction. In the Yoruba world, Oracles are generally referred to as Divination-Omisi. An Oracle is, therefore, an object that, when used to ask a question and perform an action, will give the person being consulted a response in the form of an answer.

The word Omisi is used to describe any object (which can be either human or non-human) that serves as an instrument of divination. Omisis include stones, sticks, shells, turtle shells, etc. These objects have been known to have been used by the Yoruba people before Babalawos were created. The Babalawo's role is to interpret the omi's responses and give a report or a prognosis to the person who consulted.

After the death of Babalorisa, his siblings were left to take his place as the keeper of the gods. This is where the Babalawos come in. According to their belief, they are supposed to take on this role once they reach adulthood. If one does not achieve this status before death, there are people who will continue to practice divination for them after their death. As a result, divination continues to be practiced in Yoruba communities even after the creation of the Babalawo order.

Divination amongst the Yoruba people can be traced as far back as their creation. It is said that Orunmila, their creator, was the first diviner who founded the art of IFA (Ifa literature). The practice of divination in Yoruba land also existed before the Babalawo order was created. Divination for this race is believed to have been performed by babalorisa, or Babalawos, who were well versed in Ifa and its related sciences. They were also literate and versed in the arts and sciences of their culture.

Babalorisa was initially an order of priests within the Yoruba society. They performed different roles such as keeping records for the gods, watching over funeral rites, narrating their people's myths and legends, supervising births, marriages, and deaths, among other things. Babalorisa were also known to be well versed in various runes or charms that would be used for divination.

The Yoruba people themselves had their own interpretation of divination and how it was practiced. The diviners among this race would use items such as stones, shells, and sticks to perform divination. Their interpretations and way of doing things differed from those of the Babalawos.

There is an overwhelming belief among the Yoruba people that the power of their gods is so strong that they can be contacted through divination alone.

Divination is a practice of discerning the future or the unknown by divine, intuitive, or prophetic means. Divination can be broken down into systems that use various ways of understanding what a questioner seeks from a diviner.

Tools for Divination

The Diloggun is a cowrie shell divination system, and to get started and get results, you need to follow some precautions. In Santeria, an important figure is the Oba, who represents a divinatory priest who must have a bag of cowrie shells to be used for divination. The number of cowrie shells each Oba possesses depends on which divination is performed. For divination in honor of Eshu, a messenger of the Orisha, 18 are used, for other Orisha 18 or 16 cowrie shells.

Divining Bone

Cowrie shells are used in divination, and each small shell contains a group of indefinite motifs etched on its surface. These signs contain many interpretations, which can be interpreted by a practitioner or by an Ifa priest, thanks to a small bone, a fundamental tool for divination, and which can be considered a watershed between good and evil.

Cleaning

Typically, the tools used for divination come. This ensures that all impurities are washed away from objects, leaving them clean for use by the Orishas to respond to humanity.

Cleansing and purification are very important in divination. Impurities must be washed away from objects, and these precautions allow a greater and pure connection between the Orisha and humans. It is purified and consecrated through blood sacrifices and prayers.

The time of divination

Time is an essential aspect of divination. According to the Yoruba people, Osun, the main Orisha of divination, is present and operates only during the day and with the heat of the sun. For this reason, divination takes place exclusively from sunrise to sunset, and at other times of the day, it may have no effect.

Divination Platform

Diloggun is defined as the divination system and consists of throwing cowrie shells and subsequently interpreting the signs created by them. The divination platform where cowrie shells or even kola nuts are thrown is usually a table, raffia rug, wooden tray, or cloth, usually white. This tool is used to create a sacred space for divination purposes.

Dowsing Cloth

Whenever any divination is done, different preparations are made, and sacred clothing is used. The diviner cloth used as a platform is essential. It can be red or white in color, depending on the type of divination being performed, and is often decorated with cowrie shells. Fortune tellers must be stripped of any superfluous objects (necklaces, rings) as these could affect and compromise their divination.

Efun

Represents Ire in divination, i.e., a blessing. It is a sphere made up of pulverized eggshells held in the palm of the hand.

Ota

Represents Ofo in divination, that is, misfortune. It is a black-colored rock object held in the palm of the hand.

DIVINATION SYSTEMS

Divination systems play an important role in all kinds of religions, and that is true of Yoruba religions as well, which have a deep connection to divining practices. These systems help people connect with the deities and answer some of the questions they may have about the universe. They also create organized guidelines for practitioners to follow, and these guidelines are passed through the generations to keep the religions thriving. Divination can come in many forms, and while there are certainly differences across Yoruban religions, Yoruban systems generally share many of the same tendencies and rituals for divination. Yoruban divination systems allow people to talk to Orishas to tap into their power and call to them for help. While some of these terms and techniques have already been discussed, this chapter will give a more in-depth view of divination in Yoruban religions.

Divination is a way to tell the future using methods that follow certain rituals, and these rituals vary by the practice of divination in use. While life may seem random and disjointed, divination shows the way it works more clearly through the integration of the spiritual realm. Many people are skeptical of divination because they believe it contradicts scientific principles; however, that does not have to be the case. Rather than viewing it as superstitious, many people choose to believe that spiritual practices like divination go beyond science to explain something outside of the physical realm, which science cannot do because it relies on our five physical senses, which do not fully perceive the spiritual.

In general, divination refers to the acting of using supernatural methods to find information about life's biggest mysteries, including the future and the spiritual world. When you hear the word supernatural, you may be thinking of things like vampires or werewolves, but the world has much broader applications, and it goes beyond fantastical creatures found in storybooks. It also includes everything that extends beyond the physical world. Thus, divination is often the connection to the spiritual, the parts of the universe that we cannot explain with physical science, and we struggle to perceive these parts of the universe with our ordinary senses. Divination helps people tap into those spiritual parts of the universe as a way to learn not just more about themselves and their destiny but about the world that surrounds them.

Divination uses signs to give people vital information, and it is a sacred practice that can dictate what happens to a person. In Yoruban religions, it is often seen as a determiner of fate. Not only does it speak to the future, but it can give valuable information in hindsight that people can use to understand their past actions and influence their future actions. Additionally, it connects people to their heritage and creates a spiritual connection to their ancestors and fellow practitioners.

The divination techniques in Yoruba religions are centuries old, and they have long been used in West Africa. Their prominence has spread beyond, and they have become part of the New World through religions such as Santeria. These practices are generally practiced by priests or priestesses (Oba), who will divine on behalf of others in the religion, but independent practitioners do exist, especially for Yoruba practitioners outside of organized groups or who prefer solitary spiritual endeavors. Diviners generally require extensive training to ensure that they know all the stories and signs associated with Yoruban divination practices.

Across Yoruba and Yorba-inspired religions, divination practices are integral in the religions, and few Yoruban religions do not include divination techniques. These religions include divination practices, and what individual religions entail for divination can range greatly based on the techniques employed, the tools used, and the specific practices of the religion. It was Orunmila that showed people how to complete divination using the Ifa system of divination. Other systems of divination include Obi Meanwhile, Olodumare began divination using the Diloggun, which is associated with the Santerian religion. Thus, there are many types of Yoruban divination, each with its unique properties. Yet, there are also many common threads between the systems. A common tool among the Yoruban divination systems, for example, is the use of cowrie shells, showing how interconnected Yoruban practices are.

There are certain parameters for most types of Yoruban divining. For example, the time of day for divining is important, and it is important to only attempt divination from dawn until dusk. Prayers are also used to cleanse tools used in divination across all practices and ensure a strong practice of divination. Furthermore, whenever a person is divining, they must have a clear intention, or they may have unclear or insincere answers. A diviner should be mentally prepared for the divination, as should the person who is asking for divination. Sincereness is important, and if a person is not sincere in their request, they will not have worthwhile results, and the practice will be a waste of time.

When thinking about divination, it is vital to remember that connecting with the spiritual has many challenges. Divination is never as straightforward as you may wish it was, and that is true with Yoruba divination as well, which means that the communication humans get from the gods and goddesses is often vague or feels a lot like a puzzle. With practice, anyone can improve their divination skills and understand how to interpret the answers given to them. Though, in most Yoruban religions, divination is only carried out by highly trained religious leaders. Nevertheless, you can uncover a deeper spiritual connection when you commit to learning divination.

Despite all the rules, hardships, and complexities of divination, it can be a highly rewarding process when done properly. Divination creates a powerful connection with the Orishas, and it can help people enrich their spiritual experiences. These practices have been completed for hundreds of years, and they continue to provide fulfillment for people, and they continue to provide enriched spiritual lives for those who follow the various divination methods. In Yoruba religions, the Orishas predate time or the world itself, and they will continue long past all of us and Earth is gone. Thus, they have valuable wisdom and guidance to give through divination.

Interpreting Shells' Mouths

One common ritual in divination is the use of cowrie shells, which are typically thrown to give answers from the Orishas. Thus, cowrie shells are a highly important part of divination because they symbolize the Orishas' mouths, which means that they tell the messages that the Orishas are given. Shells have a serrated side, which looks something like a parted mouth. The serrated side is the "light" part of the mouth, which is the one that speaks, while the other side is the "dark" (sometimes called "silent") side of the mouth, which is usually shaped so that it is flat on the bottom rather than curved.

A reading starts by finding the primary Odu, or a written work that points to the meaning of the shells. The primary Odu, which is the Odu that gives the most significant messages. This task is done by evaluating the open mouths of the shells. From there, the shells will be cast further to determine other meanings and figure out certain specifics.

Most of the time, the mouths will be open, but in rare instances, all the Orisha mouths may be closed. This occurrence happens when all the serrated sides of the shells are downward. If such a thing happens, it is a terrible sign, and it would result in several cleansing rituals to try to heal the bad omen.

The answers are found based on not only how many mouths are open but also the pattern of how the shells fall. It is up to the diviner to determine the meaning behind the tossed shells. Most forms of divination use collections of works that have been passed down. These works can include poems, stories, and prayers.

Obi Divination

Obi divination is a method of divination that provides yes or no answers. Still, the answers are more complicated than merely yes or no, as this divination gives various levels of yes or no because it uses four pieces to give those answers. For example, Alaafia is the strongest yes, while Ejife is a simpler yes. It uses four (sometimes five!) kola nuts in place of cowrie shells, but in some cases, shells are used. In this process, you must throw five pieces on a divination cloth, and then a priest or priestess determines what signs are being presented to you. Often, practitioners toss the kola nuts twice to confirm responses or get more nuanced answers. This form of divination is fairly simple and easy to complete. Alternate versions of this system exist. For example, in the Caribbean and Latin America, instead of kola nuts, they usually use four parts of a coconut (which is fitting because Obi means coconut).

It's important to remember that these answers reflect one's current track. Thus, the outcomes can change with effort, but it may require substantial (or sometimes not so substantial) effort to do so. These responses are often used by practitioners to determine how to do better going forward rather than as something they are destined or doomed to experience. Divination is never a sure tell of the future, but it is instructional and highly informative.

Alaafia

When four mouths face up, the answer is Alaafia, which is a strong yes that means "yes with blessings."

Etawa

Your answer is Etawa when three mouths are up, and one is down. It means "maybe."

Ejife

Ejife is another version of yes, but it is less string than Alaafia. You get it when you have two pieces up and two pieces down. It is a more balanced yes, meaning it is a yes without the emphasis. It also represents harmony in the universe. With this answer, you do not need to throw the pieces again to be sure.

Okanran

Okanaran suggests that a positive outcome is unlikely to be reached or that someone needs to do more spiritual work to change the outcome. It is represented by one mouth up and the rest down. It tells you that you're going to have to put in a lot of effort to make a change.

Oyekun

Oyekun is the firmest negative response. It happens when four pieces are mouth down. It will usually require a person to find balance through rituals, cleanses, and handling their negative energies.

Ifa Divination

One of the most prominent types of divination is Ifa divination, which you have already been introduced to. Odu Ifu contains stories and prayers that Orunmila gave to priests, who then assured the information would be shared with many generations. It has 16 books that are then divided into 16 smaller books. In total, there are 256 Odu within the system. Listed below are the sixteen major Odu of Ifa divination because it would be too overwhelming to list summaries for all 256 works.

Okanran

Okanran suggests that someone must be persistent. It may also suggest something to do with tumult or losing someone or something important in one's life.

Eji Oko

Eji Oko suggests that there is a conflict between two people, or it could relate to one's ancestors.

Ogunda

Ogunda reflects small fights, but it also represents candor, a strong work ethic, and earnestness.

Irosun

Irosun is another one that has to do with ancestors, and it focuses on family trees, but it also relates to charitable actions.

Ose

Ose suggests things such as plenty, goodwill, and sweetness.

Obara

Obara usually has to do with finances, and it is usually related to financial gain over a financial loss.

Odi

Odi represents concluding something that one has started or earning the benefits from hard work.

Eji Ogbe

Eji Ogbe refers to bodily prosperity and longevity and that one has many blessings.

Osa

Osa marks change, and it usually refers to a big change.

Ofun

Ofun suggests spiritual enrichment and wealth, but it can also represent that something is going to come to an end.

Owonrin

Owonrin usually has to do with one letting go of the past and moving forward.

Ejila Sebora

Ejila Sebora can refer to loss, usually of a lesser degree. It can also refer to gossip or fickleness.

Ika

Ika is another Odu that suggests change, but it can also mean illness of some sort, whether physically, emotionally, or spiritually.

Oturupon

Oturupon is most linked to humbleness and bravery.

Ofun Kanran

Ofun Kanran reflects education and the act of seeking more knowledge, but it also represents tranquility.

Irete

Irete has bad associations as it is related to feeling held back or confined. It can also suggest high-stress levels or some kind of pressure, whether external or internal.

Diloggun Divination and the 16 Basic Patterns

Diloggun divination is known within Yoruban culture as Odu Orisha Erindilogun because of its use of 16 cowrie shells, which each represent a primary Odu, a work that reflects the message being given, and this is quite similar to other divination systems. A priest or priestess in the Santerian religion has training that helps them figure out what the meaning of the shells is. Due to the secondary Odus, there are 256 signs that can result in this practice, meaning that it takes significant study to understand the potential outcomes. All the signs are linked to stories that can help guide practitioners. During Diloggun readings, people can learn about the past, present, and future through the signs.

The tools of divination are important. While sixteen shells are used in divination, the Oba may have up to twenty-one shells if divining for Eshu, while other Orishas may require 18 cowrie shells in the Oba's possession. A practitioner will also need to have a diving bone, which represents the division between good and evil, which makes it an important tool in divination. An Efun represents blessings (Ire), and it is a ball of eggshells that practitioners hold in their hands. Another item held in a practitioner's hand is an Ota, which stands for misfortune (Ofo), and it is black and rocky.

Additionally, a divining platform is used in these practices to help read the signs by the shells that the Oba throws. This platform can be a white cloth, a table, a tray, or other similar surfaces. Practitioners also wear a diving cloth, which is often white but can be read in certain instances. This cloth will be adorned with cowrie shells. Furthermore, jewelry is removed before divination.

As with Ifa divination, this type of divination uses sixteen primary Odu, and the way the shells' mouths land influences the meaning of each throw. Below are the various outcomes that may occur.

Okanran

Okanran tells one not to hurt other people, and it happens with one mouth of the shell being up.

Eji Oko

In cases where there are two mouths up, you have Eji Oko, which tells you to not be hurtful or hateful towards others.

Eta Ogunda

Eta Ogunda warns against revenge and bitterness, and it is three shells with their mouths up.

Irosun

When there are four shells with their mouths open, you have Irosun. Irosun tells you not to unfairly speak badly of someone or run their information. It also tells you not to confine them.

Ose

Ose happens with five upward mouths, and it tells people not to be jealous.

Obara

Six mouths being faced upward reads as Obara, which promotes honesty.

Odi

For seven upward mouths, Odi tells you to be virtuous and to not corrupt other people.

Eji Onile

Eji Onile means you have eight shell mouths facing up, and it tells you to keep a level head and to not carelessly share the secrets of other people.

Osa

Osa occurs with nine shell mouths being upward, and it tells you to be genuine in your interactions.

Ofun

When you have ten shell mouths facing you, it indicates that you must avoid things such as cursing too much, stealing, and other similar vices.

Owanrin

Eleven mouths indicate Owanrin, which means that you should not destroy the lives of others in any way. It also suggests that you should be thankful for the good in your life.

Ejila Sebora

When twelve shells have open mouths, you have Ejila Sebora, which warns against indiscretions or tragedies.

Eji Ologbon

Eji Ologbon occurs when thirteen of the shells face up, and it tells one that they should honor those who have come before. It is sometimes known as metala.

Ika

Ika is the merinla, and it happens when fourteen shells face up. It is a warning not to spread disease, but it can also be a reminder against wrongdoing and evil.

Osbegunda

Osebegunda occurs when fifteen of the shells have open mouths. This is called the marunla, and it is linked with respecting people, such as parents, children, and elders.

Alaafia

When sixteen shells have their mouths up, your response is Alaafia, which is considered a merindilogun. What that means is that listening to the advice given by the reading will lead to tranquility and courage when standing in front of Olodumare.

Opira

While there are only sixteen shells, Opira represents when none of the shells are faced mouth up, and it can be a bad omen or a sign the reading is not accurate.

Tips for Divination

Divination can be a challenging and intimidating process, but if you keep certain tips in mind, you can get a better sense of what divination is, how to use it, and what it means in the grand scheme of things. The more you deal with divination, the more natural it will become, and you won't feel as overwhelmed as you might feel right now.

Find someone who is knowledgeable in Yoruban divination. The best way to understand divination is to see it in action from someone who has practiced it. No book can rival experiential knowledge, especially for spiritual development. This book can give you the facts you need to know to take steps towards spirituality, but you must take action to reap the benefits. Learning from wiser individuals is always a fantastic option, and it's also a great idea to find a community that appeals to you.

Remember to keep an open mind. If you don't keep an open mind, you won't get good results from divination. Part of divination is belief. If you don't think it's going to work, there's no way that you will have a meaningful connection with the Orishas. It's as simple as that. It's normal to have some doubts, and many people starting spiritual journies are skeptical, but you need to let go of the skepticism and give divination a chance. It doesn't hurt to try, so you have very little to lose and a lot to gain.

Practice focusing on your intentions. This book has already mentioned the importance of your intentions in divination, and that point cannot be understated. Just as your belief shapes your outcomes, you have to be clear about what you want and why you are seeking wisdom. Spiritual leaders can often help you with this and show you what to do to stay on track, but it's also something you can learn through techniques such as journaling, which help you process your thoughts and desires. You can work hard to do better. Just as if you slack, you can fall behind!

You always have some degree of autonomy over your fate. Remember that no matter what your reading says, there's still a chance to change the direction of your life. Use divination as constructive feedback and not a reason to give in to bad things that could happen or stop working towards positive things.

You're not going to fully understand divination ever, so don't try to. The bottom line is that divination is full of mystery that no human could understand, no matter how spiritual they are or how long they have been practicing divination. There are some things that you will never be meant to know, and don't take that as a failure or let it discourage you. Take a deep breath and see what happens. Don't try to control your experience; instead, learn to appreciate the process for what it is. When you can do this, you can channel the Orishas and gain valuable insight.

ORISHAS FESTIVAL AFRICA

Orisha festivals are an important aspect of the religious life of the Yoruba and are celebrated in honor of the deities who come down to Earth to interact with mortals. There are many important Orisha festivals in Africa, and during these celebrations, various rituals are performed, which include the burning of sacrifices, singing, and dancing.

Olokun Festival

Olokun festivals are the set of annual celebrations that are celebrated throughout Yorubaland in honor of Olokun, lord of deep waters, protector, and guardian of African souls. They are organized to venerate and thank Olokun for all the benefits received over the past year. Olokun Festivals is a community-wide event that involves many people from the state and features different types of traditional arts. Some include music, mask making, dance, and arts and crafts. The colors used for traditional clothing are blues and immaculate white. Devotees sprinkle their faces with white chalk.

The main sanctuary of Olokun is located in Nigeria in the state of Osun, and more precisely, in the Ilode district of Ile Ife. An important festival for the Edos, it takes place at the end of February, in Usonigbe, in the state of Edo in Nigeria.bThe most recent festival is held in Lagos (Nigeria), in the month of November, and attracts many people from all over Africa and also from the rest of the world.

Osun Festival

Osun Festival is a festival of the most revered, and Osun is prayed by the faithful who ask him for protection and resolution to the various problems of life. It is held every year in the sacred forest of Osun, a city in the state of Osun in Nigeria, between the month of July and August. Originally born as a religious event to venerate the goddess of the Osun River, the festival has evolved into an important cultural celebration of the Yoruba people.

It is an event deeply felt by the locals because Osogbo is celebrated as the place of the Osun settlement. During the festival, there is no shortage of typical party activities such as drinking, eating, dancing, and playing.

In addition, acrobatic performances and other traditional events are held, which also involve neighboring countries, which come to honor Osun. The most important and sacred aspect of the event is when the priests and the faithful go to the temple to pray and pay homage to Osun and to ask, also through sacrifices, for spiritual and physical renewal. Then a procession is made to the river bank where people are prayed, and food is thrown as an offering.

Sango Festival

This festival is named after the Yoruba Orisha Sango, a deity of thunder and fire.

Its main purpose is to promote the cult of Sango through arts, crafts, cultural performances, and temporary shrines erected in Sango in each of the communities founded by Ekekwe.

The festival features the commemoration of the ancestors and giving thanks for their blessings. Begun in the community alone in Ijaiye, it soon became a national celebration, held in over 50 cities in Nigeria alone. The Sango Festival is an annual festival and usually takes place in August at the Alaafin palace in Oyo. in Nigeria.

A festival is an event featuring an opening ceremony, keynote address, performances, and worship. Various groups parade through communities where temporary shrines have been built in Sango, worship it, and receive blessings and luck for their lives.

Featuring various events, including traditional crafts, music, dance, and performing arts. It also features several traditional dances such as "Ajebutter," "Agbesan," "Akutan," among others. The festival attracts many people from all over Nigeria and is considered to be one of the most popular festivals in Oyo state.

Obatala Festival

The Obatala Festival is an annual festival, and it is a cultural gathering celebrated in Nigeria and many other African countries. The festival honors Obatala, the god of life and death and the supreme creator, and begins with women in prayer, calling out to heaven, until Obatala's powers descend. It involves traditional crafts, music, dance, and the performing arts.

The festival features different types of traditional art such as mask making, dance, and performing arts. It includes a procession of worshipers dressed in white and silver jewels and of priests around the cities, where they sing and dance to the accompaniment of drums and chants in praise of Obatala.

Igbin bells are also rung, a musical instrument invented centuries ago to celebrate Obatala, and food offerings made, always in honor of him. This festival is very important to the people of Yoruba, as it is one of the main festivals that exist in their culture. The celebrations involve artisans who make traditional artifacts to use during the celebrations.

Olojo Festival

The Olojo Festival is an ancient festival celebrated annually in October in Ife, in the state of Osun, Nigeria. There are no precise dates for the first event, but it seems that the Festival was held for the first time between the 11th and 15th centuries.

It is a very important festival for the Yoruba people because it is also known as the celebration of the black race in the world. Olojo has as its meaning "the day of the first sunrise," so this festival has as its main purpose the celebration of creation, both divine and man.

It is celebrated in honor of Ogun, the god of iron and fire, to ask for luck for the year to come and for wealth and abundance in crops. Tradition has it that before the festivities begin, the reigning king will invoke prayers and perform rituals together with seven high priests. He will have to isolate himself for five days to speak with the deities who resided in the ancient city of Ile-Ife.

Throughout the period, the Ooni could only eat spiritual foods, alligator pepper, and kola nuts. Also, during this time, the high priest will go to the Oonis to perform some rituals for five consecutive days

Ogun Festival

This Festival, like that of Olojo, is celebrated in honor of Ogun, god of iron, but celebrated in the state of Ondo and also of Ekiti, in the month of August.

Ogun is the patron saint of those who use metals in their daily work, such as surgeons, blacksmiths, and mechanics, who must be revered by these categories of workers to receive favor and protection from him. The celebrations begin with the priest, who, playing the Upe for seven days, announces the advent of the new moon.

A representative of the priest acts as a messenger announcing the beginning of the ceremonies to all the faithful, and the sanctuaries are embellished for the occasion. The festival includes traditional crafts, music, and dances. During the festival, ancestors are also worshiped, thinking that the ancestors are with them again to greet them and bless their brothers. To worship Ogun, the elements used are palm oil, dogs, roasted yam, palm wine, cold water, and kola nuts.

Ogun festival has become one of the most popular festivals in Nigeria. It has become a popular annual event, and in addition to attracting local visitors from all over Yorubaland, visitors also come from other parts of Africa and different parts of Europe to visit this festival.

Yemoja Festival

Yemoja is considered the Mother of all, the source of all waters, including the rivers of West Africa, especially the Ogun River. The Yemoja festival is a celebration that takes place annually for 17 days in October, commemorating the Yoruba religion and spirituality through a full program of dance, song, and ritual festivals. The festival begins by cutting the newest yams, called Ila'su. Subsequently, sacrifices and gifts are also made to other Orisha of water, such as Oya and Osun.

During the grand finale of the Yemoja Festival in Ibadan, several groups of Orisa devotees dance to the rhythm of the drums in front of the Yemoja Temple. Inside the temple is Ogunleki, an old statue of Yemoja about 1 meter tall and over 400 years old, depicting a woman nursing a baby. The faithful sing Yoruba songs, thanking the Orishas for having given them health in the previous year and for having been able to participate in another party.

Next to the Ogunleki statue, there is a series of hollowed-out pumpkins into which sacred items are dropped as offerings to the goddess, such as dried kola nuts where people have spoken prayer words to Yemoja.

Outside the temple, accompanied by the music, women dressed in white carry pumpkins on their heads. In each pumpkin, there are different things, cooked beans, corn, fruit, polenta, prepared for the Orisha. Participants follow the procession of the arugba, the pumpkin bearers. Their destination: the nearby river. Their purpose: propitiation and prayers to Yemoja.

A procession of Arugba and devotees begins, which will take them along the river to make offerings and other prayers to Yemaja, to thank the fortunes of the past year, and to propitiate what is to come.

SANTERIA

Santeria is a blend of Catholic practices and African traditional beliefs, which rose to prominence in the 17th century and has been a part of Cuban society ever since. Nowadays, it is a lot more popular than Catholicism on the island—Santeros transcends Catholics by eight to one. Cuba remains the religious hub of Santería, but the faith now spans several other countries, including the U.S.

Santeria is actually not a set of beliefs. It is a "syncretic" religion, meaning it blends aspects of a variety of diverse cultures and faiths, although some of these beliefs might contradict one another. Santeria blends influences of Caribbean tradition, elements of Catholicism, and West Africa's Yoruba spirituality. It evolved when African slaves were taken from their homelands during the Colonial era and subjected to forced labor in Caribbean sugar plantations.

Santeria is a passably intricate system. This is due to blending the Yoruba Orishas, or divine beings, along with the Catholic saints. In some parts, African slaves learned that worshiping their ancestral Orishas was a lot safer if their Catholic owners were convinced that they were worshiping the saints instead – this led to the tradition of overlap between the beliefs.

The Orishas were regarded as messengers between the humans and the divine. Priests summon them through a variety of methods, such as possession and trances, divination, ritual, and as well as sacrifice. To an extent, Santeria involves magical practice, even though this magical system is founded on interaction with and the understanding of the Orishas.

Key Points of the Santeria Belief System

Santeria survived for centuries despite various efforts to eliminate it. It even became popularly known as Santeria as Africans initially recognized the likeliness between their Orishas and some Catholic Saints.

Many of today's adherents that had the branches of the religion's foundation in Cuba prefer to call themselves Lucumi adherents, and Santeria is also referred to as La Regla De Ocha. This roughly translates to 'the rule of the Orisha.'

All over the US, Latin America, and Europe, Santeria is widely practiced today. Despite its wide practice, religion still faces immense fear, misunderstanding, and mystery. To clear the air on many of these beliefs and lay the fears that wrap themselves up with this religion, we'll be examining the main elements of the Santeria religion.

Followers of Santeria Believe in Just One God

Just as many of the modern belief systems, the practitioners of Santeria believe that there is only one God, Olodumare, the creator of all. Santeria is not a pagan religion; neither is it polytheistic. It isn't an animistic religion either. Many people believe Orishas are God, which is the main reason for the widespread confusion. The truth is that the Orishas are not God.

They are parts of God that manifest around us and our natural world.

Every person is regarded as the offspring of a particular Orisha. Hundreds of Orishas exist, and some are more revered than others. Some most revered Orishas include Esu, widely known as the trickster deity, Sango-the king of drums whose strengths are thunder and lightning. He was once the King of Oyo.

Other revered Orishas include the god of all blacksmiths and iron, Ogun. He is widely known as a warrior. Yemoja is the deity who governs the oceans and is a mother to everyone. Obatala owns all uninitiated heads, and he stands for patience, justice, and wisdom. He is widely regarded as a peaceful King. Osun, the deity of calm waters, guards all things that make life beautiful. Oya is the queen of the market who guards the entrance of the cemetery.

There are many more Orishas, and each of them has its own unique character and importance.

Santeria Followers Worship Their Ancestors

A big emphasis is placed on ancestral worship in the Santeria Belief System, just as in most other African religions. Worshiping the ancestors is an integral part of Santeria, and before any ceremony is held, libations and prayers are raised to the ancestors. While this is going on, the names of deceased family members and religious stewards who are now regarded as ancestors are mentioned.

In addition to these practices rooted in African beliefs, the practice of Misa Blanca and Espiritismo in Europe has been integrated into Santeria's practices. There is no ranking in this context because everyone is believed to have the capacity to improve his or her personal know-how as an individual. Songs are sung, and prayers are offered to call the spirits to communicate with those at the ceremony.

A French educator named Allen Kardec, who was born in 1804, founded this practice. He held the opinion that humans were spirits that lived in a physical body and that we were indeed spiritual and not physical. He was of the belief that each person has his or her own guardian angel specifically assigned to them and charged with caring for them. In return, they must be accepted before they can look after us.

Divination

At one point or another in their lives, Santeria followers would find themselves at the house of Dilogun-the Divination having sixteen cowrie shells, or Ifa. These two are the primary and most rated types of Divination within the Santeria belief system.

There is a probability of two hundred and fifty-six different signs popping up in just one reading. There are many stories and parables connected to each of these signs, and reading informs the worshipper of the place they find themselves in life. It entails the past, present, and future. The worshipper whose reading was being done would be offered advice on how to achieve a balance in their personal lives, the path they should tread regarding their personal relationships, social, work, family, and spiritual matters, and practical recommendations on ways to achieve their dreams. These devices are not final as the onus rests on the worshippers to take them or not. It is a matter of free will, and the worshipper is entitled to free will.

Another Divination system is Obi. In this system, five kola nut pieces are thrown, and it is an easy form of Divination used by worshipers whenever they want to talk to their Orisha.

Initiation Is One Year and Seven Days

During Initiation, various ceremonies are held for a preliminary period of seven days. This is then succeeded by a year of stringent code of conduct, including wearing white apparel, beads, and sacred bangles. During the one-year period, the members undergoing initiation must stay away from members who aren't being initiated. They are not allowed to shave, wear makeup, drink alcohol, or eat with others at the table. That's not all. They are also not permitted to visit crowded places, shake hands or hug anyone, go out at night, collect things directly from people, walk barefooted, take pictures, or attend parties.

They are only permitted to eat and drink from a special personal bowl, spoon, and cup, which they are required to carry around at all times. Keeping pure is also expected of them, while they must take their time to study and understand the Orishas and their advice. Their heads must be covered every time, as the year signals the kick-start of a new life in which they have been reborn. At the end of the year, the newly initiated members will continually follow certain restrictions and taboos for the rest of their lives. Every member has different taboos applicable to them, and a newly initiated Santero is given the title Iyawo.

Two Concepts Are Vital to the Fundamental Beliefs of Santeria

The first among these theories or concepts is Ase, which has Brazilian and Cuban variants spelled as Axe or Ache. All variants are pronounced as A-she. Ase is the force of life in all humans; it is the productive energy bestowed on everyone by Olodumare. This energy is the breath of the powers or force of life within us, and we cannot live without it. It empowers us to create and grants us the wisdom to discern tough things. In simple terms, Ase is life, and there is no life without it.

The other concept or theory is Iwa Pele. This translates to a compassionate and good character. Both initiated and non-initiated Santeria practitioners need to understand the concept of Iwa Pele. One must live with good character to have a purpose in this life as we are spiritual beings that oversee living the best lives that we have been given. Our works should revolve around scrutinizing our flaws and ironing them out. It is of utmost importance to be conscious of being a person who has a compassionate character and working toward being a better person. When this is done, the flow of energy changes around us.

Having titles such as Santero or Babalawo amounts to little or nothing if such a person doesn't measure up to the standards of Iwa Pele.

Santeria Isn't Witchcraft

Many people are scared or skeptical about Santeria because of their association of Witchcraft practices with Santeria. Santeria is not witchcraft, neither is it in any way related to witchcraft. Santeria does not study spells or teach how to use spells to harm anyone or otherwise. Only misguided people who are void of adequate knowledge believe that Santeria can be used for sinister purposes such as winning the lottery, harming an enemy, or making someone love them.

Everything about Santeria entails living the best of your life that Olodumare gave you. Admittedly, worshippers do several things, such as wearing sacred necklaces, having a spiritual bath to protect themselves, giving offerings or sacrifices to Orishas or their ancestors, or using herbs to protect or cleanse themselves. None of these practices is related to witchcraft.

Animal Offerings

Animal sacrifice in Santeria has always been a subject of debate. Offerings or sacrifices to Orishas or ancestors usually include things such as candles, fruit, flowers, water, or edible food items. When a reading is done, the advice that would follow may be to improve or change one's behavior, and only in rare cases would an animal be requested as an offering. Regardless of this, the animal offering makes up part of the practices in Santeria.

Contrary to common belief, animal sacrifices aren't as harsh as these animals are eaten and not wasted. The animal for sacrifice is slaughtered and prepared in the same manner as Jewish and Moslem practices for slaughtering Kosher or Halal meat. Usually, prayers follow the sacrifice, and the people in attendance eat the animal.

Their Temple - The House of a Santeros

Generally, there is no church or a specific place where Santeros gather for worship. As a result, their houses serve as temples. There is no Bible or law guiding the Santeros, but each person is given personal advice by the Orisha they adhere to. They use Divination systems as a guide and rely on their ancestors for further help and counsel. The Divination system gave out moral tales and stories that were orally passed from one generation to another. In modern times, books containing these stories have been published.

Different Songs Accompany Different Ceremonies

Every Santeros must know the songs that apply to different ceremonies as a matter of importance. This will enable them to join in the songs and create a viable Ase. Ceremonies are public, and anyone can attend, but non-initiated members cannot go close to the drums as they have to be at the back. Everyone can sing as it plays a major role in improving the energy in the atmosphere. An Orisha known as Ana lives in the sacred drums, and this Orisha is responsible for the speaking of the drums.

The Orishas descend in a ceremony known as Tambor. In this ceremony, initiated priests are turned to vessels, which are then inhabited by the Orishas for a short period. This happens so that the Orishas can bestow knowledge and good counsel on everyone who is present at the ceremony.

In modern times, many cultural projects have refurbished the Orishas song tradition. Despite this, the rhythms and cultural meanings remain unchanged, but the drums are no longer sacred. These songs are nice songs, and their renderings are deep. Their cultural meanings arose basically from an existing spiritual tradition.

ORISHAS IN OUR DAY

You may be wondering why all this information about Orishas really matters when Yorba religions began so long ago. You may think, "Okay, all that is interesting, but what does that have to do with my present life?" Many people have similar reactions, but there's so much enrichment that you can have by having a continued appreciation for the Orishas and Yoruban religious rituals.

Orishas often seem like outdated deities to many modern people, but that is not at all the case. These spirits, in a wide range of capacities, can still be relevant to people of today. While many people may have misperceptions about Yoruba religions and not understand Orishas, that does not invalidate the power of these deities. Modern-day people around the world find connections through the stories and rituals of Orishas. Some people have a more serious connection than others, but in all cases, a deep connection can be found in Orishas. Even if you aren't sure whether you believe in them or not. Give Orishas a chance, and as you experiment with them, you will start to find the path that is right for your needs as an individual. Don't close your mind to this idea until you have time to process the information in this book and attempt to build a personal connection.

The first thing to mention is that belief in the Orishas are not dead. Across the world, Yoruba and Yoruba-inspired religions remain present. These types of religions are the seventh most common type of religion in the world, and millions of people still practice what has been detailed in this book. Thus, no matter what your intentions are reading this book, hopefully, you can take some time and contemplate how Orishas can be present in your daily life.

Again, you don't have to rush into anything, and you're welcome to process this information at a pace that works for you, but remember that Orisha worship is a highly viable spiritual choice for lots of people. You may think that you need to be initiated into the religion to engage with Orishas; however, that is not always the case, and there are people who deal with Orishas without all the strict practices and more organized groups. Spirituality exists on a spectrum, and how you want to celebrate that part of you depends on what gives you joy and balance. History shows how this works. For example, as you know, Santeria combines many traditional Yoruban practices with Catholicism. Thus, the evolution of Orisha worship and spirituality is acceptable and welcome.

One of the best parts of Orishas is that they can connect you to your ancestors. The rituals and stories of the Orishas have been passed through the generations, and they continue to connect the past with the present and the future. There's no denying the power of so many years of history and connection. Orisha worship was an original religion of Africa before colonizers came in, which shows how rich the Orisha culture is. Think of how nice it would be to carry on the information and spiritual beliefs that have existed for so long. Orishas have been passed through the generations and can continue to be passed on, which is an amazing thing.

Yoruba religions have a great power to create community. Communities that celebrate and worship Orishas are some of the most vibrant and helpful communities that you can engage with. You can find people who have similar troubles and concerns as you do and learn how to mitigate those concerns through religion.

Orishas can help you find focus in your life. One of the most amazing things about discovering Orishas is that they can give your life a direction when previously you weren't quite sure what you were doing. If you feel lost, finding a spiritual practice that appeals to you can be one of the greatest discoveries.

By understanding Orishas, people can be more in harmony with themselves and their world. A big emphasis of Orishas is balance and harmony in the universe, and this is something that we could all use in our lives.

Orishas create a deeper understanding of the universe. When you only understand the world based on its physical elements, you're missing out on many of the deeper connections. When you find a spiritual connection, you find greater meaning in your life. That meaning can help you discover not only what you want from your life but what gives you the most meaning as a human being. It's natural to feel lost sometimes, but when you have a guide through the Orishas, it's easier to be found.

Yoruba religion can bring spiritual peace. If you feel like your world is too full of chaos, the Orishas can give you guidance. They are filled with the answers of the universe, and they serve as resources for people who most need their guidance. They speak to people, and all you have to do is listen to what they are saying. When you learn to listen to the messages of the Orishas, you uncover truths that help you defy the chaos that likely drives you crazy. No one likes chaos, and while it is somewhat unavoidable, you can find order within that chaos.

There is so much of yourself that you have yet to understand. No matter who you are, there are elements of yourself and your world that are still such a mystery. Getting to know the Orishas can demystify some of that and help you be more at peace. Life is scary, but with Orishas, it makes more sense, and you can get a better sense of your role in the world rather than feeling like a tiny, meaningless part of it.

One amazing thing about Orishas is that they are not perfect beings. Yes, they are higher powers, and they have many strengths that humans don't have, but they also have flaws and egos that can get in their way. Thus, people can relate to them, and by relating to those who rule over us, we can start to understand why we are the way we are and realize that we too are part of the universe and are influenced by the Orishas whether we want to admit that we are or not.

Orishas dictate how the world exists and operates. They teach people how to be more in tune with the universe and all the parts that are within the universe. Take some time to imagine how the Orishas can be part of your world. It may be hard to imagine at first, especially if you are super new to the idea of the Orishas, but with some contemplation, you might discover that the divine can take your life to new heights and help you find parts of yourself you didn't know exists. The Orishas are still perfectly alive and relevant to today's world, and people all around the world will continue to celebrate them for years to come.

CONCLUSION

The Yoruba religion is the main religion in West Africa. It is also present in parts of Brazil, Cuba, and other Caribbean countries. The faith has many different aspects to it, which are all part of developing a deeper understanding of Yoruba culture. The Orishas are fundamental figures because they are the deities who interact with humans in order to ensure their well-being.

The Yoruba religion believes that spirits move amongst the living, so they pray to these deities at times. They believe that natural forces are their enemies, so it is important to be on their good side. They also worship the deceased, who are the ancestors of the living. They have a system of sacred animals, which are very important to this religion; they believe that all these deities can be seen as manifestations of one Supreme God.

There are several types of Orishas, each with its own function, but all of them represent chieftains, which is the highest level in the Yoruba society. They also created personages, which are believed to be deities in human form.

The Yoruba religion means "the way of the ancestors" or "the way of the Yoruba people." In Nigeria, we have the largest group professing this religion, over 19 million people, out of about 25 million individuals.nThe other part of the population follows other religions such as Christianity or Islam. However, the Yoruba use different forms of Christianity and Islam because they are mixed with their traditional religion.

This religion considers rituals and venerations important for an intense and complete connection with the spiritual world and, in particular, with the Orisha. It is a religion that considers its ancient traditions fundamental and essential. Many people will follow the Yoruba religion for personal reasons and for social acceptance and will also try to convert new members to this faith, illustrating the many virtues and positive sides of this religious belief.

Over the centuries, the Yoruba people have emigrated with their culture and traditions to different parts of the world, influencing the countries of emigration in many ways. In South America, between about 1500 and 1600, a group of people, originally from the territories of present-day Nigeria and Togo, migrated from West Africa, bringing with them the traditions of the Yoruba religion. Around 1520 AD, they moved to the Bahamas and to Cuba in 1695 AD. The Yoruba people developed their businesses to support themselves, mainly in the fishing and agriculture sectors.

Thousands of Yoruba emigrated to the United States, and today they are the third-largest African ethnic group in the country. According to recent estimates, around six million people of African descent in the United States are returning to Africa due to education and job opportunities outside the continent. However, according to some recent studies, around sixty-two percent of Americans of Nigerian descent are believed to be born in America.

A new generation of Yoruba-Americans is forming, and the children have come under intense pressure from parents, relatives, and other members of the community to conform to traditional customs. The number of women practicing religion is on the rise, but divorces are also on the rise. Yoruba living in New York mostly follow traditional customs than those living outside the city limits. It has been observed that Yoruba females are more conservative in their lifestyle, while Yoruba males have great freedom. The Yoruba are known for their great hospitality, are very kind to strangers, and are generous even without necessarily getting something in return.

They believe in spirits and believe that if a person does not have a spirit to guide them through life, they will be troubled by many problems. There are several Orishas who protect the faithful of the Yoruba religion and represent a beacon, a light in their daily life.

In order to have serenity and peace, the Orisha must be prayed to and given sacrifices to them. They can represent salvation on many occasions, and their divine help will often become precious.

Many Yoruba believe in the afterlife and think that when people die, they will exist in another world. Their religion tells them that if a dead person does not make his way in this life or if he does not make peace with other living beings, then they will go to hell. We can say that the Yoruba are unique and have kept many of their traditions and beliefs, keeping their culture as pure as it was hundreds of years ago. The younger generations have been influenced by Western culture but have done their best to keep the old and sacred traditions alive.

9 781803 618739